Every Life Tells a Story

AN ANTHOLOGY

by
Eugen V. Rosu

Every Life Tells a Story – *An Anthology*

Copyright © 2022 Eugen V. Rosu

Paperback ISBN: 978-1-958405-16-1
eBook ISBN: 978-1-958405-15-4

Library of Congress Control Number: 2022917038

Interior Design: Amit Dey

This book is a work of fiction. Names, characters, accents and dialects, places, businesses, organizations, and events are either the product of the author's imagination or are used fictitiously. Any resemblance to an actual person, living or dead, events or locales is entirely coincidental.

All rights reserved. No part of this publication may be reproduced or transmitted in any form or by any means, electronic or mechanical, including photocopy, recording, or any information storage and retrieval system, without permission in writing from the author.

Publisher: Spotlight Publishing House
https://spotlightpublishinghouse.com

www.eugenrosu.com

Every Life Tells a Story

a Story

AN ANTHOLOGY

by
Eugen V. Rosu

Goodyear, AZ

Preface

This anthology took almost a year to make. It started with the idea of storytelling and how much our lives are influenced by the stories we hear.

Throughout my pastoral experience, I heard and told many stories. Two significant aspects of the stories' impact happened during my time as a university chaplain and mainly as a hospital chaplain. I learned that people had stories to tell about their needs, pains, and joys, and no one made the time to listen to them. The other staff member had limited time in a patient's room, so the only person who could spend more time with the patient was the chaplain. In the university setting, the students sought the chaplain, and at times they would come to talk with us during our daily presence in the student lounge. Many of the stories that I have heard over the years marked me and inspired me to start this project.

Authors write the stories you will read from nine to 80 plus years old. They all share their moments of truth. These stories relate to events that took place in the writer's life. Others relate to sites with a magical impact of transformation. Other stories relate to life's challenges and the struggle to overcome them. These stories are about parenting, childhood, faith, fighting against all odds, places to visit, and mysterious happenings, all of which are about life. Life as it happens.

The purpose of these stories is to send the vibes from the writer's heart to you, the reader's heart. These stories will inspire you, uplift you, and motivate you. The stories will bring you closer to the authors, and I hope they will encourage you to see that you are not alone; someone else went before you through similar experiences.

I hope that these stories will make you laugh, jump out of your chair, offer help to someone, or say a prayer for someone you know who needs it. Regardless of how you feel, enjoy this book written with love for life.

Eugen V. Rosu

Acknowledgments

This book was made possible to be brought to life due to the generous support of all authors included in it. A big "Thank you!" goes to my wife, who showed patience and encouragement as I was working on the book.

I am grateful to the patrons of his book – Cheryl Davis Robbins, Simion and Carmen Coca, Demetrios Deliz, and William Anastopoulos - who brought this book to life with their generous financial support.

Eugen V. Rosu.
March 11, 2022

Contents

Preface v
Acknowledgments. vii
The Gift of Life by Eugen V. Rosu 1
God by Angelina Nădejde 3
January by Asma Nooruddin. 5
Sinai by Alina F. Bajan 7
Beloved by Dana Fodor Mateescu 9
Postcard to Skywalker by Dana Fodor Mateescu 11
A Mindset by Ana Maria Rosu. 13
The Second Chance by Silviana Carter. 15
Ace by Em Sava. 17
The Woman That I Am by Martha Jijia 19
Women Who Changed My Life by Part I by Vesna Lucic 21
February by Asma Nooruddin 23
The Meaning of Words by Luminita-Elena Stoenescu. 25
What's Your Carrot? by Ronald Rock 27
The Beauty of Spring by Mara Viliga. 29
Omu' by Silvia Grigore 31
Midsummer by Em Sava. 33
The Spiritual Father by Eugen V. Rosu 35

Dear People by Angelina Nădejde 37
Feed the Birds by David M. Oancea 39
Beginning by Em Sava 41
March by Asma Nooruddin 43
Martisorul – The Spring Trinket by Răzvan Gabriel Mateescu. . . 45
Jerusalem by Mara Viliga. 47
Sunrise by Ronald Rock 49
Enisala – A Love Story by Dana Fodor-Mateescu 51
Amazing Prayer by Cornel Todeasa. 53
Doctor Apostol by Silvia Grigore 55
Where Are You, Mother? by Angelina Nădejde 57
Acacia Trees by Luminita-Elena Stoenescu 59
A Young Girl's Journey by Felicia Ramirez-Perez 61
The Beauty of Foolishness by Mariana Alexandrescu 63
Lost in Los Angeles by Eugen V. Rosu 65
The Best Day by Chris Dorris. 67
Dad's Jokes by Eugen V. Rosu 69
Being Grateful by Mara Viliga 71
Without you by Angelina Nădejde. 73
Guilty by Mariana Alexandrescu 75
The Note by Luminita-Elena Stoenescu 77
Little Things by Em Sava 79
Life is Precious by Felicia Ramirez-Perez. 81
Mothers by Dana Fodor Mateescu 83
Our Mothers…Candles Burning with Tears by Angelina Nădejde . 85
My Buni and I by Dacia Snider 87
May by Asma Nooruddin 89

Elena by Dana Fodor Mateescu 91
For you by Angelina Nădejde 93
Adina by Silvia Grigore 95
Prayer by Ana Maria Rosu July 15, 2019 97
Team Building by Luminita-Elena Stoenescu 99
Forced to Escape by David M. Oancea 101
A Cool Car by Eugen V. Rosu 103
Life's Lesson by Silvia Grigore 105
Surprised By Life by Silviana Carter 107
Father's Letter by Mariana Alexandrescu 109
Be Considerate by Luminita-Elena Stoenescu 111
Sleepwalking Candy Sales by David M. Oancea 113
Happiness by Anastasia Ciuntu 115
Where Did She Go? by Ronald Rock 117
Parenting Without Manual by Dana Fodor Mateescu 119
The Wind of Change by Emilian-Ciprian Ene 121
The Gift to Receive by Chris Dorris. 123
Easter Light During the Pandemic by Luminta-Elena Stoenescu. 125
Heroes by Eugen V. Rosu 127
Scars of Early Life by Silviana Carter 129
"Love Your Neighbor." by Chris Dorris 131
A Woman Like Me by Martha Jijia 133
June by Asma Nooruddin 135
Happiness for Me by Angelina Nădejde 137
Take an Extra Minute by Luminita-Elena Stoenescu 139
A Great Day by Ana Maria Rosu (9 years old) 141
Life as it happens by Kay Huber 143

Above All, We Must Pray! by Cornel Todeasa 145

Needs by Em Sava 147

Don by Luminita-Elena Stoenescu. 149

My New Dress by Dana Fodor Mateescu. 151

Funny Crepes by Emilian-Ciprian Ene. 153

What Am I Doing Here? by Mariana Alexandrescu 155

A Corner of Paradise by Eugen V. Rosu 157

July by Asma Nooruddin 159

A Place to Wander by Mara Viliga 161

Inspiration by Brenda Whillock 163

"Again and Again, in Peace, Let us Pray to the Lord!"
    by Cornel Todeasa 165

A Delayed Gift by Luminita-Elena Stoenescu. 167

Enchanted by Elena Lupu 169

Just for You by Angelina Nădejde 171

Moved to Tears by Ronald Rock. 173

A Son's Love by Luminita-Elena Stoenescu. 175

My Ancestry by Dana Fodor Mateescu. 177

Sticking to Principles: To Play or Not to Play?
    by David M. Oancea. 179

Love Conquers All by Stamatula P. Kretsedemas. 181

Clear Sky by Chris Dorris. 183

Fear Not Death by Cornel Todeasa. 185

The Happy Bubble by Purvi Desai. 187

Beauty Standards for Today's Woman by Anastasia Ciuntu 189

Never Make a Woman Cry by Angelina Nădejde 191

Women Who Changed My Life by Part II Vesna Lucic 193

OMG by Ronald Rock 195

Stranger's Generosity by Luminita-Elena Stoenescu 197

I Am Driving! by Stamatoula P. Kretsedemas 199

Open Door of Opportunity by Luminita-Elena Stoenescu . . . 201

My Roots by Ioan Rosu 203

August by Asma Nooruddin 205

The Bean Dish by Eugen V. Rosu 207

Flowers by Angelina Nădejde 209

Being Happy by Andrei Cristian Mateescu 211

Journey to My Ancestral Roots by David M. Oancea 213

Overcoming Adversity by Brenda Whillock 215

A Thankful Decision by Lori Foley-Jacquez 217

The Day I Got My Dog by Ana Maria Rosu 219

The Opportunity For Change by Bassam Matar 221

Friendship by Eugen V. Rosu 223

The Other Face of Justice by Silvia Grigore 225

A Temporary Guest by Luminita-Elena Stoenescu 227

Nettles by Luminita-Elena Stoenescu 229

Alone In An Ocean of People by Mariana Alexandradescu . . . 231

Summer Day by Em Sava 233

The Woman and Her Flowers by Luminita-Elena Stoenescu . . . 235

Let's Go! by Elena Lupu 237

Constantin by Eugen V. Rosu 239

A Good Man by Angelina Nădejde 241

A Miracle of Healing by Cornel Todeasa 243

Making Time by Cornel Todeasa 245

Modern Slaves by Em Sava 247

October by Asma Nooruddin 249
Mother's Tattoos by Silvia Grigore 251
Fathers Lose Babies Too by Ronald Rock 253
The Forgotten Book by Luminita-Elena Stoenescu 255
The Magical Box by Dana Fodor Mateescu 257
Divorce, Hatred, and Rebirth by David M. Oancea 259
Worship, Not Entertainment by Cornel Todeasa 261
The Circle of Life by Lori Foley-Jacquez. 263
Katerina by Eugen V. Rosu 265
I Wanted to Become a Priest… by Ronald Rock 267
Why Not! by Emilian-Ciprian Ene 269
Overcoming Fear by Luminita-Elena Stoenescu 271
Serenity by Ioan Rosu. 273
The Badger—A Winter Story by Eugen V. Rosu 275
Silvia by Dana Fodor Mateescu 277
The Game That Mirrors Life by David M. Oancea 279
Being On Time by Cornel Todeasa. 281
Paleontologist by Eugen V. Rosu 283
Of The Emigrant by Em Sava 285
A Wave of Vain Questions by Angelina Nădejde. 287
Guilt Versus Gratitude by Ronald Rock 289
But Watch for the Blind Spot by Cornel Todeasa 291
Don Calistru by Eugen V. Rosu 293
Joe's Bakery by Eugen V. Rosu. 295
Grateful Beyond Words by Ronald Rock. 297
Morits by Dana Fodor Mateescu. 299
Be Still by Cornel Todeasa 301

Wonders of Nature Through a Magnifying Glass
by David M. Oancea 303

Not From A Distance by Cornel Todeasa. 305

Holidays by Em Sava 307

The Woman by Angelina Nădejde 309

Grandmother Maria's Wisdom by Silvia Grigore 311

A Wasted Life by Ronald Rock 313

Time to Relax by Elena Lupu 315

Linden Flowers by Eugen V. Rosu 317

A Voice to Remember by Eugen V. Rosu. 319

December by Asma Nooruddin 321

Don't Be Surprised! by Em Sava 323

We Live Virtually by Angelina Nădejde. 325

Mary and Martha In Us by Cornel Todeasa. 327

Christmas Presence by David M Oancea 329

Today by Asma Nooruddin 331

Canadian Christmas by Em Sava 333

Where Do I Meet the Sacred? by Ciprian Ciuntu 335

Snowflakes and People by Luminta-Elena Stoenescu 337

April by Asma Nooruddin. 339

Friends by Angelina Nădejde 341

A New Beginning by Em Sava. 343

Curiosity at the Creek by David M. Oancea 345

Summer Rain by Ioan Rosu. 347

Meet the Authors 349

We Appreciate Reviews!. 355

The Gift of Life

Eugen V. Rosu

There I was, standing between my wife's bed and our daughter's crib, two hours after her birth, taking pictures and showing them to my wife. I remember my wife asked me something about the baby, and my answer came out with a squeaky sound. My normally baritone voice sounded then like a mouse's squeak. I was afraid I might wake up the baby by using my normal tone of voice, so I tried to whisper. What changed my voice was not entirely my fear but amazement to see that little miracle I was holding.

As we tried to grasp the joyous moment in our lives, a nurse came in to check on the baby and my wife. As she was doing her job, the nurse remarked that the baby looked so much like her father. My wife and I smiled and thanked the nurse for her care. A few minutes later, the doctor came in to check on my family, and he, too, made a similar comment as the nurse before him. Before he left the room, the doctor congratulated us and assured us of his care. After a little while, a nursing nurse walked in to see how the baby was doing during feeding. As she grabbed our daughter, she remarked, full of surprise and amazement, that she had never seen a girl look so much like her father. She assisted my wife with the nursing, gave us a few tips, and left the room.

After the third visit, I thought that I had to do something for my wife. Three compliments were made to me, and my wife was not mentioned. I felt terrible, and I knew I had to do something quickly. I went to the nurses' station, and I asked if one of them could go into the room and casually tell my wife that the baby looked like her. One nurse volunteered. She walked into the room, acted professionally by checking the baby, asked my wife how she was doing, and then said that our daughter looked like her mother. I do not know if my wife was convinced.

I was glad that someone made that remark for my wife to hear, but I thought the nurse did not do it the way I wanted my wife to hear. After many years, my wife still hears that remark, but now, she accepts it with a smile and sometimes with a comment of her own.

God

Angelina Nădejde

God,
if I lived another life,
I would not miss a day
to enjoy my childhood.
I would not fall asleep without the angel's embrace
of the face of a mother and her story
in the evening.

I would only grow and flourish for whom
worth flowering.
I would beg my heart not to beat hard
at every flutter of his wing, believing
that it is love.

Gestures will hurt it,
words,
silences.
Wounded, it will have no strength
to love.
I would command my eyes
to build up tears of suffering,

and I will gladly wash them with the joy from the faces
of good people.

To the hands,
I would say to give comfort
and lift the fallen one.

I would ask my soul
humility
for it is from here springs
love,
kindness and
the beginning of wisdom.

January

Asma Nooruddin

During the winters in Kabul, my older brother forbade my older sister and me from going out into the backyard until the snow had a chance to pile up. Once it did, he would call our friends over to play in the snow. I remember how we fashioned giant snowmen and frantically built fortresses to defend ourselves from a shower of snowballs. These battles were always a thrill, especially with a dozen or so children shrieking with equal measures of glee and terror.

Once, I romped around alone in the leftover snow while my mother was out on an errand. After I came back and removed my boots, I saw that my toes had turned blue, so I started a hot bath for myself. As I was about to dip my feet into the steaming water, my nanny came to check in on me. She panicked when she saw me poised over the tub and carried me out of the bathroom to rub my legs down. According to her, if I had hopped into the bath, I might have lost my toes.

To this day, I'm impressed by the stories of the elderly women who would go to the frozen river and pick the ice until they could draw water to use for their ablutions. The fact that they would wash in freezing water just to perform their five daily prayers is a testament to their resilience and devotion to their Lord. I have never met stronger people, both spiritually and physically, outside of Afghanistan.

The Afghan boys had a tradition of keeping themselves busy during these long and harsh winters. The trees had lost all of their leaves and exposed the sparrows who perched on their naked branches. The boys would use slingshots to shoot the birds down, then make a stew out of their tender meat. I would always feel sorry for the sparrows, especially because they looked so cute when they were sitting in squat little balls, feathers puffed out for warmth. My older brother also felt a deep connection to these birds and could never bring himself to join the hunt.

The winters in Afghanistan were the coldest I have ever known. However, I remember them with so much warmth and affection. Truly, the hearts of the Afghans are as pure as a fresh bed of snow.

Sinai

Alina F. Bajan

I longed to get there. And it happened, but it was more complicated than I thought. It was, however, more beautiful than I could have ever imagined.

Before arriving in Egypt, I received clear instructions from my colleague and my Egyptian friend, Magdi. I had to have physical training, thick clothes, and proper shoes to climb the mountain. When I arrived in Sharm el-Sheikh, I only had sports shoes. I did not bring thick clothes because Egypt was like eternal summer for me. Since it was March, I thought Magdi must have been exaggerating to me. Except, he was right. The raid on Moses' Mount began at midnight, and because the mountain is in the desert, chances were that it would be zero degrees Celsius at night.

Being sensitive to cold, I panicked and started desperately rummaging through stores. But being in Sharm, the diving paradise, I could only find swimsuits, sunglasses, and diving equipment. By a miracle, I found a wool sports pullover with the inscription, "ARSENAL." Victorious after hours of rummaging, I landed at the hotel so tired that it was as if I had already climbed Moses' Mount.

At midnight, the climbing began in the darkness lit by torches from place to place. To my surprise, there were a lot of tourists. They seemed to be on the pilgrimage in well-organized groups. Most were Christians from Nigeria.

I asked, "When do we reach the top?" Magdi answered, "At 5 in the morning." "Aha!" I asked myself and raised another question, "And when do we get back?"

"At 8. In returning, it takes less time."

"Wow!" I said to myself. A question with physiological origins struck me. "Magdi, are there toilets on the way?" Smiling slyly, Magdi answered, "Yes, of course! They are the Bedouins' toilets."

"Huh, okay," I tell myself. I take a deep breath and say, "Let's go because I'm already frozen!"

Magdi answered me in astonishment, "Do you know what the Bedouin toilets are like?"

"How should I know I haven't been here before!"

Magdi said, "They are under the starry skies of the desert. See how lucky you are tonight. It's a full moon!" I was drinking water at that moment. Water came out of my nose, and I felt like I had a kidney block. I was horrified. Magdi laughed out loud.

Beloved

Dana Fodor Mateescu

Beloved,
get on my right hand and tell the death I'm gone.
Send her for a screwdriver cross,
tell her it's raining bluefish and water lilies as big as my city,
give her work, maybe she forgets about me.

Death has a dog in its mouth and on every finger.
Barks like a fool because I love you.
Let's run to the field with white shoulders, baby,
Where far means here,
Where owls have silver and alexandrite bracelets.

Honey, what's wrong with you?
Your flesh is like red melon, and you burn.
Come over! Here, we are close to the horizon.
We get to where the darkness turns upside down and screams.

It's snowing from the ground in the sky with golden tickets,
and again, I hear the angels coming out of your mouth.
Your courage has broken legs, baby.

If you're afraid, get on my shoulder, and tell death,
that I don't have diesel anymore.
But I have blood mixed with wine, and your eyes grown on my forehead
Whistle my name, baby!
I'm not afraid of anything anymore.

Postcard to Skywalker

Dana Fodor Mateescu

Yesterday, I rummaged through the closet and came across a bag where I kept my memories. In it were letters from 10th grade that high school classmates and friends had sent.

The year?

1986.

And I turned inward. I opened a door I hadn't entered in a long time and searched coldly through the small rooms of my soul. I remembered how I scrolled like an agitated goat in front of the mailbox, eager to receive the letters from the Jedi knight who moved my stars with his thoughts and the letters from another urban prince with whom I fell in love monthly.

I was so happy when I saw a letter in the mailbox. I took the letter and tore it, curious as a cat and with a beautiful fever on my face, a fever that I lost somewhere down the road.

My heart was pounding. *Tuc-Tuc-tuc-tuc*. The recipient was Dana Skywalker. Wow! Why? Do you still ask? I was a Jedi, and I didn't care much about the Romanian Post office, security, and rules.

One day, two militiamen came and asked my mother, "Comrade Fodor, who is this Dana Schi-Val-chier?"

My mother grew small and turned pale with horror. She said, trying to play it off, "I think it's Dani, my daughter."

"And give what to call Șchi-Val-chier because I can't even pronounce. How was it played? How old is she?"

"Sixteen."

"Well, at the age of sixteen, should she still be playing games? Isn't she in high school? Bring her here!"

I went. I had been behind the door listening to everything. They asked me the same questions. I explained to them that everything was just a joke. I told them about *Star Wars*, *The Empire Strikes Back*, and *Return of the Jedi*. They looked at me with wide eyes and gaping mouths. They couldn't believe it. They didn't understand.

In the end, they told me that someone from the apartment building notified the police and took a letter to the Militia. That explains why I didn't get an answer from Cristi.

Then, they instructed me not to receive any more letters with the name "tha caiualcher" because it is illegal. This seems to be reactionary. It is not Romanian, and I will have to account for it.

My mother scolded me. My father broke another switch with his fist. All our switches were now broken.

In three days, things calmed down, but I still got letters with the same name, Dana Skywalker. The "militiamen" never came back.

A Mindset

Ana Maria Rosu (9 years old)

I was getting ready for the tennis match. It was my first time participating in a tennis tournament. Walking toward the tennis courts, a thought hit me. *Will I win, or will I lose?*

I asked my father if I could win. He replied that I could because I could do anything if I put my mind to it.

When I was on the tennis court, I saw my opponent and remembered what my father had said to me. I got ready—left and right. I hit the ball, and I won the last match.

Then, the coach pulled us in for the final score. Sadly, I did not win the tournament, but I ended up winning second place. I learned from that event that never lose hope and always try your best. You never know what you can do until you go out and do it.

The Second Chance

Silviana Carter

My brother, Stefan, is a strong guy with muscles and tattoos. He is almost 41 years old, and he loves his son very much. He named his junior son after himself, Stefan. The ladies from the town hall registry said, "Really? Do you want us to write Junior on the birth certificate?" Stefan said, "Yes, that is what I want." He told me there was something to convince the ladies.

My brother was imprisoned in 2007 for about five months because he used drugs. He sold my father's only fortune to get money, his books! Stefan sold all kinds of things for drugs. When we were younger, my mother died. Stefan was 13 at the time, and he did not know how to cope with the situation. We were both depressed.

He used all sorts of things for about 10 to 15 years. It's tough for me to understand. When I visited him and my father, Stefan lied to me that he was clean, and sometimes he managed to fool me. I heard about a church you can go to with desire for nine Tuesdays, and on the tenth Tuesday, you go with gifts and leave some of them there. On the ninth Tuesday, I went with the desire for my brother to quit drugs, and nothing happened. Then, I said in my mind that God has nothing else to do but count my Tuesdays and then fulfil my wish! And then I went for a year and a half.

After this time, my brother's girlfriend called me and told me, "Your brother was arrested in Ploieşti because, in Târgovişte, they knew him at all the pharmacies." At that moment, I said to myself; there is NO God! I prayed for my brother and look at what was happening!

After a week of staying there, my brother sent me a letter. My sister! There is a God! I did not believe in him, but He is there! I have given up drugs!

He came home after five months and fulfilled his biggest wish: to have a baby! And he had Junior!

Ace

Em Sava

My son and I wanted to have a dog. My husband opposed the idea for many years, and when we thought we had lost the battle, he surprised us. He bought a three-week-old golden retriever for Christmas and placed it under the tree. When I saw him, so tiny and cute, in a basket with a big red bow around him, it was love at first sight. He looked at us, anxious. It was the happiest Christmas we have ever had in Canada. I had a new member of the family, apricot-colored, soft, and cute. I named him Ace, and he became our beloved friend. A lovely friend but with terrific grips and very sharp teeth.

He had Handsome Boy syndrome and grew up overnight. In a few months, we woke up with a big but stupid dog who still behaved like a puppy and overturned us when he jumped on us with joy.

He gnawed at everything from doors to slippers. On walks, he dragged us after him because he was always in a hurry. We did not walk Ace, but Ace took us where he wanted. And he begged. He begged for comfort from everyone. As someone passed by on the street, he took a standing position to caress him, and if the person happened to pass by without noticing him, he would grieve and make the long face of a troubled man.

Once he got off the leash and for hours, we struggled to bring him home. He thought we were playing with him, and he ran us all over the park and into the streets. He was the most walked and trained dog, but he was a naughty one. He was holding on to mischief. If we were not careful, shoes became perforated by his teeth, and all the doors and nets bore the imprint of his sharp teeth. If we tried to leave him alone in the yard, he would get upset and bark all over the street, indignant that we were in the house, and he was outside.

He did a lot of tricks, but he was the most beloved dog.

The Woman That I Am

Martha Jijia

Occasionally I like to shop at a particular store, but before I walk into the store, I like to have a nice cappuccino at a nearby coffee shop. Because that is my favorite place to drink my coffee late in the morning, I got to know some of the customers, who are as regulars as I am. I prefer my corner, where I can enjoy my coffee without anyone walking by me. As I savor my coffee, I like to read something new. Sometimes I read a book and sometimes an article. No, not articles from those popular magazines that you can find in any waiting room. Interesting ones.

Among the regular customers, there are women from their late twenties up to my age. What is my age? That is none of your business. Some of them come from a local yoga place from a nearby gym. All of them are dressed, and each time I see them, they have a different outfit, in yoga pants and some type of top to show their upper body. Some of them look great. Others just enjoy the clothing. Some of them do come from yoga or the gym. Others just to show off their new acquisition.

One day, one of them, one closer to my age, came to me, and after the casual introduction, she offered me a brochure from the yoga place. Along with it, she gave me a business card from a place that sells yoga outfits. Before she went back to her table, she told me that once I got in the yoga outfit, I wouldn't look for any other clothes. And how good I would feel about myself in those clothes. I thanked her politely, and I smiled at her.

Finally, we women got to a point where we look good and feel good about ourselves because of some clothing pieces. How degrading that such advice came from a woman. She really identified herself with those clothes. She thought of herself as being better, better than she was before, or better than others who do not wear those things. I am comfortable being a woman the way I am; I do not need clothing to define me or to give me a state of being. And to all of you who define yourselves through clothing, I have two words to say to you: "Namaste bitches!"

Women Who Changed My Life

Part I

Vesna Lucic

Growing up in Sarajevo, I worked at a bank. My work was sort of repetitive and predictable. The house where I grew up was filled with the creative work of my mother. My mother was a clothing designer. She had an exceptional talent and was able to create anything with her hands. If you can imagine it, she would be able to make it. People would say that she had "Hands of Gold." Sadly, my mother died suddenly from a brain aneurism at the age of 41. I was only 16 years old. My life changed forever.

I owe everything that I am or hope to be to my angel, my mother.

I was very much drawn to art, and my imagination was precise. Fashion, color, texture, shape, and emotion portray the person wearing that particular garment. It has been said that we dress the way we feel. This certainly applies to women.

After my work at the bank, I would go home and start creating clothing for myself and my close friends. They were almost always impressed with my work. Making clothing was a way to relax. My mind and being were engaged in a place of imagination, creativity, and beauty. Something new that has not been created yet, excited my spirit. I was in my bubble, content, happy, and alive.

Often, I would lose the sense of time and place. Fashion shows, fashion designers, boutiques, and department stores are where I would spend endless hours looking at clothing, dresses, shoes, hats, and accessories. It became my favorite thing to do. It recharged my energy and vitality. When I travel, I always look for places where clothing is sold. I was especially fascinated with hats, so I began making them. I worked to master hat-making.

Today, I am in a good place in my life. I have a beautiful house and my own business. I grow an organic vegetable garden and enjoy my health. I consider myself successful.

February

Asma Nooruddin

In 1975, when I was three years old, my family took me to Bangladesh to see my grandparents. I only have one memory of my maternal grandfather, who passed away shortly after our visit. His beard was white, and his body was paralyzed with age. I remember how my uncle gently picked him up from his bed and carried him to a stool in the middle of the room. With a large bucket of water, a bar of soap, and a bottle of shampoo, he bathed my grandfather—right in the middle of his bedroom!

It was a novel experience for me to see how the elders were cared for. I think this is why the memory stayed with me.

In those days, the houses in Bangladesh were made out of thin, tapered bricks. The walls were at least two feet wide, and the floors were made of polished cement. Every room had drainage so that the floors could be washed very easily. This was also how a simple bedroom could be transformed into a bath if necessary.

Now that I am older, I can appreciate the genius of this design. When I took my children to visit my grandparent's home, they marveled at how the rooms were always cool in the summer and warm in the winter, despite the lack of air conditioning units. I told them that this type of building could withstand a humid environment like that of Bangladesh.

A few years ago, my grandfather's home was torn down to build a modern multi-story condominium. I was sorry to see how a relic of my personal history was demolished for the sake of new development. However, there are traces of similar architecture still standing. For example, the Sixty Dome Mosque in Khulna, Bangladesh, was built in the 13th century using the same type of red brick construction as my grandfather's home.

Not only does this mosque have historical and cultural importance, but it also has spiritual significance as a sacred place of worship. I am happy the Sixty Dome Mosque will be preserved as a World Heritage Site for future visitors to admire. Just as my grandfather was once honored and treated with respect by the younger generation, I hope those who come after us will treasure the rare and distinguished monuments that have managed to survive the passage of time.

The Meaning of Words

Luminita-Elena Stoenescu

I often think about how people use all sorts of words without understanding their meaning and significance. Words have power. They have spirit. They have energy. Words are irreversible.

Every word gives birth to something in the mind and heart of the one who hears it. Words give birth to thoughts, feelings, ideas, and understandings. Sometimes, they are true, and sometimes, they are not. Words are creative and can be destructive. Words soothe souls but can also hurt them.

Some words leave no room for interpretation. They are straightforward, profound, and complete. If I think of the word "faith," I realize it is incomplete, but if I add "working faith in love," the meaning becomes more profound.

I now remember the word "proud," and I found that people often use it in all areas. "I am proud of my daughter." "I am proud of my country." People gave it a positive meaning even though it has a negative connotation. Pride is of demonic origin. Pride is the root of all evil. People no longer shy away from pride because they use the word pride positively. Positively They do not penetrate its meaning and energy. The opposite word of pride is humility. It has a divine quality, but it seems to have disappeared from people's lips.

People no longer ask for forgiveness. They apologize. The verb "to forgive" is on the verge of extinction. I often use "sorry," a simple word. Do we find in any prayer the verb "to apologize"? No! But we say, "Lord, come back to me!"

And the word "luck" has nothing behind it. What exactly is luck? An illusion. God is the One who cares for us, the One who gives. You can quickly tell the superficiality or depth of a person by the words he says, the answers he provides, and the questions he asks.

Father Tada in Serbia often said, "As your thoughts are, so is your life." Thoughts are stringed words that have a spirit behind them.

What's Your Carrot?

Ronald Rock

The phrase "carrot and stick" is a metaphor for persuading someone to do something by offering them a reward or punishment. The idea originally came from a story in which a farmer enticed a hungry donkey to pull a heavy load up an ever-steepening hill by holding a carrot in front of him on the path. With the reward just out of reach and the stick being used as a means of motivation if needed, the donkey slowly made its way up the hill.

Many of my patients suffering from complex surgical or medical conditions requiring hospitalization face an uphill battle. They have endured numerous surgeries, painful procedures, and endless treatments. At times, they suffered alone. With the addition of a pandemic, the isolation has been overwhelming for my patients.

The idea of recovery as a reward may seem like an impossibility. It's no wonder patients become depressed and no longer willing to participate in their care. They cannot see the end to their situation.

What motivates me as a caregiver is to help my patients find their "carrot," or their own personal motivation for the reward of living, if not for themselves, then perhaps for someone closer to their heart. The carrot could be a person, a place, a disposition, or an event. It could be anything. Once patients find their carrot, they engage in their care and truly become an inspiration to me.

What they can endure is nothing short of a miracle.

Outside of the hospital, these patients have influenced and inspired me when it comes to my own life. In situations that appear daunting, whether it concerns family, finances, relationships, career choices, or a multitude of other hills to climb, I look for my own carrot.

Knowing there is going to be an outcome, what is my motivation to get there? It certainly makes the journey worth traveling.

What is your carrot?

The Beauty of Spring

Mara Viliga

How wonderful spring is when all still life awakens. Spring fascinates us with flowering trees that offer multiple colors, enticing us with the delicate scent of flowers, the raw green of the grass, and the chirping of birds.

In spring, the first soft flowers are like snowdrops that appear softly from under the cold earth. Later in the spring, the majestic hyacinths appear and fascinate us with their perfume and amaze us with their tenderness and scent. The radiant daffodils direct their flowers towards the sun.

Then, the majestic roses appear to fascinate us with their perfume and multitude of colors. When nature seduces us with its fragrance and the diversity of its colors, there is no other way to delight and enlighten our eyes. All still life blooms in vivid colors, and everything turns into a picture of beauty that fascinates.

No matter how hard and frosty it was the previous winter, spring comes out triumphant and delivers us its exceptional riches and charm. As spring rises after every frosty winter, our souls should rise after every hard trial we come across and find new ways to overcome.

Hope always accompanies us and gives us the strength to continue. When everything seems to be over, when it appears to us that we have reached the end of our powers, spring tells us that it is never too late to start again. From it, we learn that any beginning is difficult but not impossible to achieve.

Spring is the season of Resurrection, rebirth, joy, and hope. May spring remain forever in our souls.

Omu'

Silvia Grigore

He was 11 years old and was nicknamed Omu', or "the man." He begged all day, and, in the evening, he bought food and returned home to feed his sick mother and younger brothers like a big man. Omu' dropped out of school. He had an extraordinary gift for talking to people and telling his story. He often begged in front of the newsroom where I worked. Every time he saw me, he would come to me, and I would give him money depending on the small change I had. If I woke up early and had time, I would make him a sandwich.

One day, I was preoccupied with my thoughts after a harsh discussion with my editor-in-chief. As I was exiting, Omu' tried his luck. I don't know what came over me, but instead of giving him something, I asked him, "If I needed money, would he give it to me?"

Omu' responded, "How could I not give it to you when you have given me so much? When you're stuck, ask me!"

I rejoiced. I forgot about my boss. Does this child consider me a friend, or is he clever and flattering his name around town? In a short time, I discovered, with pleasure, that the child had become attached to me.

At the end of a football match, a billionaire and owner of the winning team had given Omu' 300 euros. At that time, 300 euros meant about as much as a minimum wage in Romania. Omu' took it with the most beautiful smile and ran in a heartbeat to look for me in the newsroom. "Look what I have! I'll give it to you because they are foreign, and I cannot use them."

Omu' did not know how much money he had or that he could exchange them. He just wanted to show me that he could be good to me too. I then realized that the child did not have the vocation of a beggar. He talked to people so that he would not be an outcast. He was only looking for a friend.

I took the money, bought some food, and took it to Omu's home. I talked to his mother and understood that they had many needs, especially the winter wood. A few days later, I exchanged the euros and bought them wood.

Today, Omu' has grown into a man. He works in construction in Italy because the salaries are meager in Romania.

Midsummer

Em Sava

It is the middle of summer, and people are on fire. The fire is in us, our thoughts, TV programs, and posts on social media that talk about the pandemic and the vaccine. The fire is also outside us, and the heat ignites the earth.

We wear masks. We hide the expressions of our hungry and hurried faces more and more. Never has humanity lived so well. People have never had so many options. But the options make us tired. It exhausts us. It makes it hard to choose. The need for a roof over your head has multiplied like a tree in huge houses with many rooms. Food and clothing flood us, jumping out of our closets. Netflix gives us too many movies. It is too much. We get tired of pressing the keys on the remote control, and we become more and more unhappy, pretentious, and hard to satisfy. We want to, but we don't know what we want.

Never before has there been so much unbelief and wickedness in the world. We are lazy. We move little, physically and spiritually. I transfer the emotions, many of them, to the virtual. It's lighter, more comfortable, and safer.

It is a hot July with tropical rains, humidity, and a desire for a breath of fresh air. A mouthful of faith.

It is evening, and it rained again. I have the window open to the garden. From the neighborhood, you can hear a song like a tear. She loves it and cries in a soft melody. Then, the music melts into the night. Happy birthday is heard! More voices. The lyrical love has shattered. Life goes on. The smile rises after each storm, and the rainbow of forgiveness emerges from the teardrop. After a few minds, the night becomes master. I listen to the silence after the rain—just a little. Fireworks put an end to the first anniversary and jumped crazy to the sky.

It is a July evening at the end of a day when the houses on my street cover their windows to keep their peace. Families settle down in their nests. I see through the windows bundles of wood, bright and colorful flowers, and rooftops that cover the lives of people on my street.

And then silence takes over. I look at my watch. It's eleven. The city closes the shutters.

The celebrated one knows that it is time for silence to enter its kingdom. The world is preparing for sleep.

The Spiritual Father

Eugen V. Rosu

I went to visit him. I knocked on the gate. Slowly, he came to open the gate. We went on a patio covered in vines. In the quietness of the day, the bees from his hives were busy collecting the pollen from the flowers. He sat on a chair across me with a small table between us, and, on it, there was a jug with water, two glasses, and two dishes with sour cherry jam. On one side of the table, there were three books piled up.

He looked as if I always remembered him, wearing a white shirt and black pants. As he sat down, a sunray beamed down through the vine onto his head. His rarified white hair made it possible to see an indentation in his skull. I asked him about that mark, but he politely refused to answer.

As soon as I went back home, I asked my grandmother why our priest had a thick indentation on his skull. The story was that in August of 1944, when the battle line broke not far from our village, the Russian army invaded Romania. People panicked. Some remained in the village. Some wanted to run away, but their running away was always in front of the Red Army. The group of people who decided to run away were caught in a small forest outside the village. The officers in the occupying army targeted the leaders of the village: the priest, the teachers, and anyone of influence. They beat the priest to the ground, where a soldier hit him in the head with the riffle. When his wife tried to protect him, she was hit with the same brutality. All the members of that group were beaten, shot at, and intimidated. Only a few had the courage to talk about it.

Father Vasile Pleot wanted to share with me, a high school student at the time, three books: The Bible, The Apostolic Fathers, and The Acts of the Martyrs. The Bible was worn out but well-maintained. I had it for two weeks. The other two books were in good shape, and when I was done reading them, he offered me The Apostolic Fathers as a gift. He was a spiritual father for three generations and was loved by all three.

Dear People

Angelina Nădejde

Dear people,
I sent my heart to search for me
the loves she lost,
out of indifference, cowardice,
or too much pride.

To apologize for
lack of love.
I sent my heart for the mornings
in which I did not cover you with the dew
of beautiful words.

I left them unspoken, dry
on my lips.
I should have told you always,
how much I love you
and that I cannot live without you.

That my life stands
Suspended from yours,
and I depend on your love

like medicine without which
I would enter
withdrawal.

I sent my heart for nights
in which I fell asleep
without realizing I'm losing
moments, feelings, life
and sometimes people.
I won't see some of them again.
I missed the opportunity
to be able to tell them
how much I loved them.

Feed the Birds

David M. Oancea

My wife and I recently watched a documentary about Walt Disney. It featured the Sherman Brothers, who created the music and lyrics for numerous Disney films. The song "Feed the Birds" from "*Mary Poppins* was said to have been Walt's favorite.

I, too, have always loved that song. For years, I've enjoyed observing birds. There's a small, wooded area behind our home with numerous birds, squirrels, and chipmunks nearby. This documentary inspired me to set up two large feeders near our backyard deck and fill them with black-oiled sunflower seeds. I also set out a suet holder and a hummingbird feeder. I discovered that certain types of birds prefer a seed mix that I pour on the grass at the bottom of the steps leading from the deck into the backyard.

We have a perfect view of the deck and feeders through the windows next to the dining table in the kitchen. It's such a pleasure to sit and observe the birds visiting the feeders and interacting with each other. The male cardinal feeds the female, as does the sparrow her young.

The hauntingly melancholic melody and lyrics of "Feed the Birds" are beautiful. But it is the image of the pigeons perching next to the Bird Woman, an old beggar woman, on the steps of St. Paul's Cathedral that reminds us that nature does not respect all classes of people. Besides the fact that she had breadcrumbs, the birds also sensed she was not a threat, that she was somehow on their frequency.

For me, there's also another lesson that relates to human interaction. The natural, physical laws of vibration and attraction are at work in every moment in our lives. Just like a radio tuned into certain frequencies that connect us to particular stations, each of us operates at certain frequencies according to our thoughts, feelings, and actions.

This lesson has taught me to be more aware and to track my own "level of vibration." I've found that I'm the one responsible for attracting positive or negative circumstances and people into my life as a result of the vibrations I project into the world. Feeding the birds reminds me of this truth every day.

Beginning

Em Sava

After diets and diets and diets, I concluded that they are all a big hoax. We fool ourselves because we lose weight to gain weight, and so on. The ads are half about food and the other half about how to lose weight. Put down six pounds, put seven back.

What to do, what to do? Ideally, it would be best to eliminate what is not good. *But what is not good for you can be so delicious.* It would be good not to eat in the evening. *But we get hungry at night.* It would help to move as much as you can. *But we get tired.* It is not hard to lose weight. *But it is hard to keep up with the damn scales.*

We know the rules—low carb, high protein, and salads galore. We know them, but we don't apply them because a theory is a theory. We'll start the new diet and fitness on Monday.

And my mouth was gilded. Look, it's the first day of the month. Yes, but it's Sunday. And on Sunday, the grass doesn't grow either. Or will this be Monday? I can imagine the stars plotting. After all, I can't give up pizza and ice cream on a Sunday. That's a dilemma. But life is a series of beginnings, and the excuse to start on a Monday, the first day of the month or year, is just a big excuse.

A self-deception.

The beginning does not have to be planned so far in advance. No moment is better than the present moment. In the end, it is an agreement with yourself, a promise that you make to yourself, knowing very well the consequences of respecting or not respecting the goals and rules. The diet can be for the body but also for the soul. You can clean up your eating habits, thoughts, and daily schedule. You can sweeten yourself with healthy things, uplifting activities, and spiritual readings. You can always want to become another you: the best version of yourself. This second is the right time to start because now begins the rest of your life.

March

Asma Nooruddin

I was thirteen years old when my sister married the love of her life. He was impressed by her poise and intelligence and approached my father to ask for her hand. That evening, unaware of the marriage talks between our parents and elders, my sister decided to play a prank on me and drew all over my face while I was asleep. She certainly had a good laugh, but I wonder what my parents thought when they saw her handiwork in the morning.

In those days, marriage was a simple matter. Families would network with trusted members of the community to look for suitable partners on our behalf. My parents received glowing recommendations for this particular young man and liked his gracious demeanor. When my sister learned of the proposal, she was very happy with the match. Thus, the marriage process moved forward.

For the wedding reception, my brother-in-law invited us to his village to introduce everyone to his new bride. My older brother and I accompanied my sister, and the rest of my family joined us later. The crowd at the reception was so large that it would have been a challenge to feed everyone using normal plates and utensils. Instead, my brother-in-law's family prepared a huge pile of banana leaves to serve the guests. The banana leaves were used as disposable plates. It was such a neat experience because I had never seen this kind of biodegradable dinnerware before.

For a city girl like myself, there were many incredible things to witness in the village. For instance, when I visited another young married woman, I saw how she had fashioned all of her furniture with the most readily available material she could find: mud. Her resourcefulness impressed me greatly. I imagine if the internet had existed back then, she would have become famous for her skill and creativity.

After seeing the ingenuity of the people of Bangladesh firsthand, my family returned to Dhaka, where my sister would settle for the remainder of her life. The humor with which she began her journey was something she carried throughout her marriage. Furthermore, as she was the first sibling to marry between the three of us, I would always learn something new from her experiences. Hence, I gained a life-long mentor in my sister and a pillar of support in my new brother-in-law.

Martisorul – The Spring Trinket

Răzvan Gabriel Mateescu

Every year, I remember a story from my grandmother, Maria Mărculescu. A former teacher from Busteni, she guided my first steps in life. We, the grandchildren, called her "maama." Some of her colleagues still taught at the local school, along with younger teachers who had once been my grandmother's students.

Every March 1st, the city was covered in a pink and sweet celebration like sherbet roses. We, the schoolchildren, made our first political and financial calculations for our town then. We decided who would get to offer the *mărțișor* and how much we should spend from our piggy banks for it. It was also a matter of marketing. The teacher had to know who the *mărțișor* was from. The boys had a tough time contributing.

"An envelope would be too mundane if you didn't stick a heart of gold polish on the back under which to write your name in calligraphy," I said.

Our teachers dressed so that their jackets looked like those of the most skilled and decorated generals. And if you recognized your gifted *mărțișor, or* a trinket placed close to a lady's chest next to her heart, it was a good sign.

My grandmother told me of a poor but hard-working gypsy boy. She told me, "On March 1 of 1933 or 1934, all the children surrounded me in the classroom to put a *mărțișor* on my chest. Only the poor gypsy boy remained in the corner of the classroom with his eyes on the ground. I asked him what was wrong with him, and he sighed. He told me his family had no money to give him for a *mărțișor*. The boy had found an old tin *mărțișor* in his house, which he had tried to clean by rubbing it with the hearth's ashes. He kept it hidden in his shirt, near his heart, not daring to offer it to me.

I hugged him and took it. He was as warm as his cheeks. I placed it on my chest, next to the expensive *mărțișor*. It shone like an invaluable treasure. His eyes rejoiced, and he smiled."

That year the boy finished the school year with honors. The child grew up, went to college, and became an engineer at the Paper Factory in Busteni. My grandmother kept that *mărțișor* for years. In turn, we remembered this dear teacher, who now sleeps her eternal sleep in the cemetery, still illuminating the path for those to whom she first taught.

Jerusalem

Mara Viliga

My thoughts turn to the fascinating Jerusalem. The city is laden with history and spirituality, the heavenly spirit of the three Abrahamic religions: Judaism, Christianity, and Islam. Conquered, demolished, and built, Jerusalem was reborn every time.

Worshiped by millions of people around the world, every stone of Jerusalem tells a story. In the center of the city is the towering fortress, a fortress that fascinates you with its walls and houses. The winding, narrow streets are home to Levantine aromas and cultural mix.

Jerusalem is a fascinating city, a city that bears witness to the tumultuous and fascinating history of the East. It is a city that captures you at first sight and arouses your curiosity to discover its history and mysteries. The city imposes itself through its walls, through its imposing buildings full of history.

It is a vibrant city with a rich history and culture, a wonderful city waiting for you to tell your story. It is a city full of tourist attractions, historical monuments, and places of worship for any denomination. Still, in addition to all this, it is also a city with an impressive number of shops and markets where you will find all kinds of goods. Its winding, narrow streets with shops on either side remind you of ancient times when city streets were just as crowded and lively, where merchants negotiated prices and closed deals. But besides all this, it is a city of contrasts and religions, a city full of spirituality emanating magical energy.

Regardless of the faith you belong to, each of them is a spiritual center that calls and urges you to pray. Even if sometimes its streets can be very crowded and noisy, it is a force that charges you with energy.

Jerusalem is still towering today and waiting for its visitors. Let us have a little Jerusalem in our souls.

Sunrise

Ronald Rock

Every morning, I head east and then north to work. I travel the same streets, listen to the same music and drive in the same rush hour day after day, year after year. The only thing I could count on changing enroute was the sunrise and what it would look like. Each morning, I look forward to driving over the road's crest to see what the next sunrise will bring.

One morning, I felt something a little different in the sky as I drove up over the crest. The skies seemed brighter than usual in the east. Dawn had broken, but the sky in the rear-view mirror remained dark and bleak. Oh, but in the east, the sky was changing by the second. From behind the fluffy scattered clouds that barely concealed the sun, rays of sunshine streaked upward as they scattered into the sky. From behind the thinned clouds, a flaming blend of glowing yellow and orange light tried to escape.

In the minutes that followed, the sun's rays pierced into a sky, blending into light blues and deep purples. The clouds began to evaporate as the sun slowly inched higher. The sky that stretched across the horizon had become a light pink, blending into a brighter blue by the second. As if standing guard, the trees were black and silhouetted against the sky. Their naked branches caused the sunlight to pulsate as I drove past.

By the time I arrived at work, the beauty of the sunrise was overwhelming. The colors became more vibrant as the sun continued to climb slowly. The bleak sky to the west had finally awoken and accepted the sun's reaching rays transforming it from black to gray to blue. Once the sun finally cleared the horizon, its colors, like the clouds, vanished into the brightest blue sky.

I was blessed this day to see a sunrise I would never forget. As with every sunrise, a new day comes along with the opportunity to seek out the beauty in life.

Enisala – A Love Story

Dana Fodor-Mateescu

I would never have reached the Enisala Fortress if I had not gotten lost on the way to Babadag, but in life, nothing is accidental.

When the storm subsided, I saw an older woman on the road sprinting through the rain. She was small, thin, and carrying a raffia bag. The rain had caught her.

"Where are you going, Auntie?"

Shivering, she looked at me with eyes like wheat in June, neither green nor yellow but alive like flames. She warmed up and tried to sell me fish. I told her I would have liked to, but by the time I would have gotten home, they would have been spoiled.

"Can you take me to Enisala?" she asked.

She got in the car with her fish swaying in the sack. When we passed the fortress, the rain fled into the sky

"What a beautiful fortress!" I said as I took pictures.

"If you give me three cigarettes, you'll tell yourself a story!"

Interested, I gave her half a package. She lit one and inhaled deep. She started as if spinning with a secret key.

"I am called Stefka. I'm 86 years old, beaten on the edge. I'm agile. I work. I don't give a damn about women who are fat, ugly, and lazy." The older woman's face spoke more than her mouth.

She said that an ancestor of hers, a Genoese soldier, lived in Enisala and fell madly in love with a local young woman. The young woman was grazing with goats when they met in the evening when the sun fell between the hills. One night, bad luck hit. A commander surprised them. The soldier was shot on the spot, but the young woman escaped.

From that moment on, she didn't say another word as long as she lived. She was a shadow of tears. Her mother married her to a Bulgarian man. Oddly enough, all the children she gave birth to had the eyes of a Genoese. Nobody knew why nor how. The Bulgarian man beat her to break her. He eventually killed her. But their children lived to this day. They all took with them, like a trophy, the incredible color of the Genoese eyes.

The Enisala Fortress was built in the 14th century, after which it was included in the defensive system of Wallachia. Today, the fortress of Enisala dominates the surroundings like a queen in the sky while its defensive walls hold many, many secrets.

Amazing Prayer

Cornel Todeasa

Praying for others is even better than praying for ourselves. Prayer gives the people for whom we pray great joy.

The centurion from Capernaum knew the power of praying for others when he asked Jesus to heal his ill servant (Matthew 8:8-13). The servant benefitted from his master's prayer, for the Lord made him well. The woman of Canaan prayed with amazing faith for her daughter. Jesus said to her, "'O woman, great is your faith! Let it be to you as you desire.' And her daughter was healed from that very hour" (Matthew 15:28).

"The essence of prayer is the spiritual lifting of the heart towards God," said St. Dimitri of Rostov. When we pray, we plug into the awesome grace and power of our God.

When we pray for others, we stop placing our selfish needs in the center of our conversation with God. For those moments of prayer, we overcome our selfishness by turning from our concerns to the needs of others.

Praying for others is like girding ourselves with a towel and washing their feet, as the Lord did it unto his disciples. He guided us to do the same by saying to his disciples, "If I then, your Lord and Teacher, have washed your feet, you also should wash one another's feet. For I have given you an example, that you should do as I have done to you," (John 13:14-15).

When we pray for others, we expend ourselves, for, in prayer, we give our love to others. But when we give of ourselves, we gain. By spending our love, we make it grow. The prayer for others is an expansion of our humanity, for it helps us to overcome the boundaries of this physical life.

Prayer is like planting seeds of love, which God will make germinate and grow. What's most amazing is the fact that the seeds of our prayers grow circular roots, linking us to God first and then to the people for whom we have prayed.

Our prayers for others return to us via heaven, measured, checked, and increased. As our almighty Father has promised, "Give, and will be given to you: good measure, pressed down, shaken together, and running over will be put into your bosom. For with the same measure that you use, it will be measured back to you," (Luke 6:38).

Praying for others gives us spiritual joy and makes us and those for whom we pray uncontested winners.

Doctor Apostol

Silvia Grigore

When my brother was hospitalized, I went to visit him every day. The orthopedic surgeon, Dr. Apostol, who operated on him for hip osteoarthritis, was always there. He ran all the time, slept in the hospital, ate in the cafeteria, and did something unusual for the hospitals in Romania: he did not receive a salary!

Every day, my brother would tell me what the doctor was doing.

One day, he saved a street man from death, who had fallen drunk and broken his leg. The case was severe because the man was in an alcoholic coma and had an open fracture. There was a risk that until the alcohol was removed from his body, the wound would become necrotic, and his leg would need to be amputated. The doctor managed to get him out of the coma and anesthetized him. All of that was done in record time and to the despair of the nurses who had the task of disinfecting and preparing the man for an operation, who had not been washed for months.

Another time, he operated on the hands of a monk wounded by a tree branch. After the operation, he was always interested in whether the man of God was well cared for, given that he could not use his hands. Woe to the staff, whoever neglected this patient!

He was very polite to the families of the sick. He told me not to spoil him because he does not rob people to heal them. He avoided operating on the rich because he did not want to sell his grace. He was called the doctor of the poor, and because he was different from the corrupt system, he was not much loved by his colleagues. He left me his phone number in case a poor man ever needed help.

Three years later, an acquaintance needed a hip osteoarthritis operation. I called Dr. Apostol, but his mother answered. "My son is no longer in Romania. He immigrated to France and worked at a large hospital in Paris. He hadn't planned to leave the country, but he wasn't made for this system. He had fairness in his blood that bothered many. At one point, they wanted to stage something to get rid of him. When he realized he was being hunted, he left. He is very popular in France."

This remarkable man had a hard lesson to learn in the country where he was born. Sometimes, no matter how much you want to be helpful, you have to resort to individual salvation. And I, from all this time, have learned that any personal salvation is a collective failure.

Where Are You, Mother?

Angelina Nădejde

I look for you, mother,
but I find you
only in my dreams.

I see you beautiful and sad as a willow,
who cries of pain,
on her knees
because of sin.

You locked your joy with a padlock of suffering
when you left me
in a moment of wandering
through life.

I gave him the first word
an angel,
and I took the first step
just to hug him.

He caressed my forehead and soul
with God's wings of love.

I believe I have my father's eyes in tears of guilt
and your smile, which
you lent to me first, mother.

And since then, I have searched for you.
I want to give it back to you
and to thank you
because
you left me to the Light!

Acacia Trees

Luminita-Elena Stoenescu

We lived in a village surrounded by acacia forests. My grandparents rejoiced every time they saw us at the gate, smiling and full of eagerness.

The days were complete. I didn't know boredom. I heard that once we get bored only when we do not feel love and do not find fulfillment in what we do because we lack the people we love and who are not with us.

It wasn't like that with my family. In the village, my grandfather was a potter. He often took us with him through the forest to look for sticky soil suitable for pottery. We gathered and trampled it until it flattened like a wagon wheel. We cut pieces from the earth with a sickle to search for pebbles. We sifted the small rocks out of the earth until they became as delicate as pretzel dough. We saw how a piece of damp earth placed on the potter's wheel took the form of a vessel that was then fired in the stove to become a jar. These containers were used to store cold spring water. We used bent corn leaves as a jar stopper.

As my grandfather worked on his pottery, my grandma wove carpets and sewed pillows. Just thinking about those days fills me with emotion. I can still smell the room and hear the fire burning. I can see myself watching my grandfather deliver his clay pots to the awaiting stove.

Sunday was the day when we bathed in the sun. We sat on blankets in the shade of the mulberry tree listening to the songs of birds and blowing wind. As I walked through the village, I greeted every person I saw. For those who I saw again, our responses to one another were just as welcoming as though we had seen each other for the first time.

In the garden, I walked barefoot with the goats. I was not afraid of thorns or the geese milling about. I took a bucket with me when I picked blackberries and took care that the animals did not enter people's gardens.

In the village, I did not know anger or need. My only concern was to see my grandparents happy. That village was destroyed when local authorities discovered coal and pressured people to move. Only the cemetery and the old church now remained. However, the village of my childhood continues to exist in my mind and heart.

A Young Girl's Journey

Felicia Ramirez-Perez

Growing up in a fast-paced, large city can be overwhelming. Many times, I was a young girl in a world where many are overseen.

Elementary school was a place where physical activities overshadowed any learning in the classroom activities. I was an active and athletic girl who was typically picked over boys for team competition on the playground. This continued through middle school, and I was a well sought-after competitor. No teacher paid any attention to me even though I was just getting through and barely passing until, one day, my principal noticed my athletic ability and had an interest outside and inside the classroom.

My life changed forever. My principal saw that my competitive ability could lend itself to my ability in the classroom. He felt that if I could be challenged academically that my competitiveness would kick in and push me to do my best. He met with my parents to discuss his idea. They were apprehensive because they knew how much I struggled in the classroom. My parents and principal spoke to me about the idea. I did not fully understand as I knew academically, I struggled, But like the true competitor I am, I accepted the challenge.

Many late nights of struggling and crying took a toll on me. One day, my competitive self-kicked in, and I started to do well. My confidence level grew, and I continued to improve academically. The trajectory of my life changed that year for me. Had my principal not believed in me, I would have just been another young girl in the big city with no aspirations beyond high school.

Fast forward to today, I earned my doctorate in education. I'm now a college administrator inspiring the next generation of young girls.

The Beauty of Foolishness

Mariana Alexandrescu

"It was not God who created the Universe! Gravity and quantum theory allow the Universe to recreate itself spontaneously, out of nothing. The scientific explanation is sufficient. Theology is no longer necessary." This is what the famous astrophysicist Stephen Hawking claimed.

However, in 1998, he did not rule out the divine origin and creation of the Universe. "If we had a complete theory, it would be the supreme triumph of human reason, and then we would know the mind of God." Hawking returned with a statement in force of the M theory. "There is no personal God!" he said firmly in June 2010.

However, Hawking made a bitter confession on ABC News. Although he knows more about the Universe than any other human, the failure of his life remains the answer to his obsessive question, "WHY is the Universe? WHY is there something more precious than Nothing?"

The Universe was seen, in its immensity, by the skilled mind of the researcher. In the end, clinging to a branch of the Universe, lost and confused, sad in his failure to calculate in mathematical equations and artifices the greatness of the strangeness that roams the Universe, according to laws still undiscovered by scientists,

Hawking's mind left the world unanswered. He sought the answers for a lifetime.

The work of a life of research is cornered by the most straightforward question, *why?*

Fear of discovering what you hate. Fear of a strange thing called Love.

Fear of love.

Thinking of the scientist's dilemma, as a simple temporary inhabitant of the Earth, aware of my fragility, vulnerability, limits, and weaknesses, I ask myself, obligatorily and logically: why would a man put his life in the service of the destruction of Someone who is convinced that he does not exist?

Lost in Los Angeles

Eugen V. Rosu

I was in Los Angeles when a police patrol stopped me for the first time. This was before we regularly had GPS, and the only way to reach a destination was either reading a map or hand-written directions. I was very new to Los Angeles, got lost easily looking for streets, and was driving suspiciously slow. I pulled over.

A part of me thought that at least I would get the much-needed help from someone who knew the city. But a part of me feared being in unanticipated trouble.

I opened the window, and the officer informed me that I was stopped because I was driving too slowly. I explained that I was new to the city, needed to visit one more parishioner, and was lost.

When I said "lost," he started laughing. Then in a good spirit of humor, he said, "Father, if you are lost, what about your flock?" I recognized his excellent sense of humor and asked for help. He offered to guide me on a few streets and then gave me directions on where to turn to reach my destination.

After we parted, I could not stop thinking about what had happened. To be stopped in traffic in a new city by an officer who had a good sense of humor? Was it possible? For an immigrant, this occasion was puzzling yet, at the same time, encouraging. I was not in a country where the police accused and punished drivers who got lost and slowed down traffic.

To this day, I don't know if having me follow him to my parishioner was part of his duty, but I firmly believe God sent him in a difficult moment.

Who knew that angels could show up in uniform?

The Best Day

Chris Dorris

It was a ritual that I started about a year and a half ago, and I'm surprised it took me that long to start.

This is what it is. When I wake up each morning, the first thing I do is make a declaration. And the declaration is, "this is the best damn day of my life!"

Now, there's a mantra for this: *Create the state, don't wait.* This means I am creating the state with intention. Imagine the best damn day of your life. How do you feel? Pretty darn good.

Here is the thinking behind this ritual. Why wait for something in the world to happen when you simply decide to put yourself into that euphoric, enthusiastic, and inspired state? These high-grade states activate all forms of intelligence. When I wake up and make the declaration, and trust me, some days, it is harder than others to have it be true. The important thing is I don't bail. I never bail. I do the work to have it be true.

When I can have myself be in the decision that this day, from the outset, is the best day of my life, I have created an emotional state. A high-frequency vibrational state. That then maximizes the probability of miracles occurring. Or said differently, that those high-grade states maximize the probability of me co-creating miracles during that day.

Those high vibrational states maximize the probability of me inviting other people to do the same, to join me in those elevated states.

As a life coach, the biggest mistake I have observed human beings make in the pursuit of their desires and who they want to be is putting unnecessary time in between themselves and those desired outcomes.

Create the state. Don't wait. Experiment with that ritual. Wake up. Write it on your bathroom mirror. #BDDOML. It best Damn Day Of My Life. And do the work. As soon as you wake up, decide that this day, without waiting for anything to happen, is going to be the best day of your life. And go about your day with that vibration in that state and watch yourself effortlessly create miracles.

Dad's Jokes

Eugen V. Rosu

When my daughter was about three, she challenged me to a game of jokes. It was fun, and I learned many jokes about the chicken who crossed the road. I thought there was only one version with the chicken crossing the road, but I learned about numerous versions over time—each with its flavor. Hmm, chicken with a different flavor, now this is a good joke.

Scrambling to find jokes for her age, I came up with a new one. "What does the horse say to the grass? Hay!"

My little girl immediately told me that that could not be a joke because a joke has a particular structure, and she explained to me what the construction of a joke looked like. I was shocked. She learned all of these detailed instructions from kids' shows. I tried to explain my joke, but I thought it wasn't as funny as I initially pondered it.

It has been several years now since we started telling jokes, and we still have fun. The chicken crossing the road is still the star of my daughter's jokes, but with different outcomes. I could challenge her now with puns, which might have been a little advanced for her. I was wrong because she was always one step ahead of me.

Whenever I try something new, she asks me if that was a "dad joke because it was bad." Now, she remembers the old joke with the horse and tells me that she couldn't understand it at the time because it was a dad joke.

Dad's jokes or not, we are still entertaining each other with riddles and enjoy a healthy laugh. Each day is a new day for jokes and sharing funny things that we come across. I occasionally tease her about the chicken jokes, and, unsurprisingly, she always has another one. Then, she warns me about teasing and how she is always prepared to tease me back.

I laugh as I write because these moments are fabulous.

Being Grateful

Mara Viliga

One day, as I was riding in a taxi, the driver started a conversation about his problems. He confessed to me his gratitude to God for healing his wife, who had been on the verge of death.

We realize how little time we spend being grateful for all the gifts God provides to us. We always find reasons to complain, either because of a desire that has not yet materialized or for many other reasons that often have nothing to do with us.

Our thoughts are channeled in a multitude of ways. It is too easy to lose sight of what the most important gifts are, the gifts that have been given to us in our life. No matter how good or bad we are, we must aim to live it in the best way possible.

Life is always surprising and gives us small joys to discover and cherish. By focusing on what life offers us and thanking it for its delights, we will see that we have fewer and fewer reasons for dissatisfaction, and our lives will slowly change for the better.

When we are children, we enjoy the smallest things and cherish the smallest joys that life offers us. But when we focus too much on our daily problems, we lose sight of the little things in life. And when life gives us a chance, we must try to find the strength to grow and learn something from it.

Life is always full of surprises, and small joys accompany us everywhere. All things come at the right time!

Without you

Angelina Nădejde

My soul
does not belong to me.
It belongs to those who are
close to me.

My soul lives through you,
receives light
from your eyes,
the warmth of your hugs,
and kiss from your lips.

It is connected and dependent
forever
to your life and love.

I believe it has the colors of the rainbow,
because you painted on it
your feelings.

It bears in it a joy
and sadness,

quiet and restless.

Like the seasons
it blossoms
from spring to summer
to rains of tears
and nostalgia
in the autumn.

He gets dressed
Festive in winter
and carols through mountains of snow
full of hopes
giving and giving again
love.

Guilty

Mariana Alexandrescu

I had a close relative. A forty-two-year-old male relative. I lived near him, but I didn't stay connected. I wish we could have kept in touch.

A family is valuable. The well-maintained and well-nourished ties between relatives weave a vivid and multicolored fabric work of strength, power, and support. We are there to help each other in situations, good and bad. I know this, but often, my introverted nature and defensive attitude are not allies in my actions.

My relative had no brothers. His father left when he was a child, and his mother abandoned him, too. His aunts tried to help with his loneliness and alleviate the responsibilities he had. They left him, too.

About two weeks ago, I found out that this relative had to pass a difficult life test. With no close relatives and all kinds of worries, I realized how lonely and abandoned he must have felt. How helpless and tired! How hopeless! How without anyone! How lost!

If I had stopped for a moment to sit in his place, I would have heard his cry for help, and maybe I would not have seen his demise.

Yes, he perished. He had died frighteningly fast, sick with loneliness and clinging to life.

My worries and burning priorities, like insurmountable mountains, appeared to me suddenly insignificant.

I am guilty. Because I could have done something to reach out to him, and I didn't.

The Note

Luminita-Elena Stoenescu

One late autumn day, I was sweeping the dried leaves in the front yard of our house. My husband had gone to the neighboring country for work. The house was recently built in an isolated part of our plain village. It sat in front of a dense forest.

A passerby greeted me while I was outside. After talking for a while, he asked me if I could give him work to do. The passerby explained to me that he had many kids and needed money. I listened to him patiently with compassion in my heart. At the end of our conversation, I told him I would talk with my husband about it. I asked for his phone number and told him that I would call him later to let him know, regardless of whether we had work for him.

After a phone call with my husband, he thought it would be good for the man to come by and finish the pavement in front of the house. The next day, I went to call the passerby. However, I could not find his number on my phone. I realized that during my conversation with the man, I did not press the "Save" key and forgot to save the number properly.

After a few days, I found a note on the gate that said, "I'm waiting for you to call me as you promised me!" That was all the note said. I felt guilty and helpless, so I wrote a note that said, "I would call you, but I don't have the number anymore. Please write your number here again." I tied it to the gate with a string.

The days went by, but no new messages appeared. The note hung on the gate for a long time until rain and wind destroyed it.

I was sorry to upset the man. I realized that careless little gestures, no matter how unintentional, could trigger unwanted reactions. I thought of how the man must be disappointed and of how he might not understand how a woman who wanted to help him was now silent and provided him no help in his moment of need.

Little Things

Em Sava

I have never liked long hair, even if it is a sign of femininity. Maybe it comes from my childhood when my mother, who was excited to have a daughter, dressed me very nicely and made me mowers. They were beautiful. I'm not saying they weren't.

Testimony is the multitude of pictures taken on all occasions. There were two things I didn't like, though. One was that it pulled my hair. And second, it made me waste time I didn't have. I had other things to do, and I was born impatient. So, when I finally got the freedom to decide, I cut it as short as I could. Boy.

I felt good, and I liked that my hair care was so easy. Of course, growing up, I approached all kinds of cutters and colors, but I never wore them for a long time. The exception was the pandemic period when all the hairdressers were closed, and my hair grew and grew. I was proud of it because it was long and thick. It just wasn't practical at all, so when I could, I went back to the convenience of easier-to-handle hair.

Our time is so precious. We choose to spend it on what suits us. We choose what to compromise on, what we want and do not want, who we want to be diplomatic for, and who we want to spend time with.

I felt light and happy when I left the hairdresser and my chopped-off hair behind for two wigs. It was not a big deal to get a haircut. All the sensations that came with it created a state of well-being, of regained freedom.

And I remembered a phrase I heard somewhere in a movie, "*When you're upset, change your look.*"

Life is Precious

Felicia Ramirez-Perez

The sound of a loved one's last breath. When you hear that a family member has cancer, your first thought is death. Cancer ends in death, right? The type of cancer will determine how one's journey will go.

I had the privilege to be alongside my aunt during her battle with stage 4 breast cancer. This was a very challenging time for our family because she was the first in our family to be diagnosed with cancer. I was at work when I heard the news. I could not move or speak when I got the news. It felt like a blow to my abdomen, and it took my breath away. When I finally got to see my aunt later that day, she was motionless. I went to her side and looked into her eyes, and I could see no hope in her eyes.

It felt like my life had changed forever. Over the next few days, I could see her life slipping away. We had not even returned to her doctor to learn of her treatment, yet, she had already given up.

At that point, I knew I had to help.

I knew I needed to be her strength. The only way I knew how to reach her was through Christ. My faith was not strong, and I was raised in more traditional and ritual religion. I lacked a true relationship with Christ. I came to my aunt one night and shared that I was ready to dedicate my life to Christ. At that moment, I saw something in her eyes change. She looked at me with astonishment and said, "You will need to give Christ your heart and not your mind. To be free mentally from questioning and dissecting this journey."

Christ led the journey from that point on. Miracles we witnessed and were part of were beautiful. Once the veil was lifted from my eyes, God allowed me to be free of living in this world. My aunt's journey with breast cancer ended just short of five years, but I know that was longer than any doctor or person thought she would live.

Where man stops, God continues. "I Can Do All Things Through Christ Who Strengthens Me" (**Philippians 4:13**).

Mothers

Dana Fodor Mateescu

Mothers laugh like a white sky. Mothers are soft. The smell of her crepes topped with cherry jam protects you like an umbrella from the rain.

Mothers are golden rains who do not cough at night for fear of awakening their children from sleep. Mothers sleep tormented so that you have more room in bed when you have a fever. They are happy when your temperature drops and you say, "I'm thirsty, Mommy!"

Mothers cry on the inside when you hit them. You don't see because her smile hides everything like a pink light

Mothers have courage. They are fighting your pain and your fears against all those who want your river.

Sometimes we come out victorious. Sometimes not.

Mothers fall asleep standing up. We swallow bread at night unless we can't because you are unwell.

Mothers are like rainbow trout. They swim against the current and shine wherever they are. Mothers carry unimaginable pains but laugh out loud if you ask them why they have tears in their eyes. Mothers are sighing and windy. Mothers are blue.

Moms keep you in her arms for hours when you are little, and your tummy hurts badly. Her voice is like a wind that cuts through the leaves.

They know how to call for peace.

Moms vibrate with longing when you are away.

Mothers say YES when everyone else says NO!

Mothers endure thirst, hunger, and cold. Mothers never have cravings but satisfy yours.

Mothers always kiss your tears, which burn like acid. Mothers can't stand the crying of their children.

Mothers are patient. And beyond their lives, you wish to become just like them when they leave.

Our Mothers...
Candles Burning with Tears

Angelina Nădejde

Allow me to measure
A mother's pain.
A child who goes the distance leaves his mother lonely.
All she has left are days of longing
and nights that hurt.
Look into the eyes of a watchful mother of a
sick child.

You will dive into the depths of an ocean
laden with fear and waves of sadness.
The soul fused with prayer burns
continuous.

Stop and feel for a moment
a mother's pain for her son
who has departed into his world of dreams!

She is a bird with severed wings who wants

to raise her chick from the swamps of time
and save him.
Rivers of despair and helplessness
flow through her marrow.

Be for one night, the mother of the unborn baby
Now among the angels.
Listen to her cry in the night and count her
sighs!

She was left with her life drained.
Look at the face of a mother who lost her child.
She just waits for the passing of time.
In every child that passes in front of her, she sees her
lost baby.
She exists with the burden of a remaining life
to live.

Stone sheepfold silently waiting for the passage
in the afterlife.
All he had left was the burning candle of faith
with tears and hope of meeting in the world
from beyond.

My Buni and I

Dacia Snider

My Buni and I were home alone. The house was quiet, and I could hear everything. It was about 9:30, and I was almost finished with a reading assignment. I heard Buni murmuring. I peeped around the door, and she was sitting in her chair praying.

I approached her, and when she finished her prayer, she told me a story I would never forget. When she was in the hospital for the second time, she said to me that she had crazy dreams during the night. It began a few nights before when she dreamed that she could not die until she saw Mother Mary. At that moment, she saw the icon of the Holy Mother. The colors were different shades of beautiful navy with silver sparkles. She turned around to tell the girl that there was Mother Mary, but she was gone. She could still see Mother Mary holding Christ and telling her to believe in prayer.

She showed me exactly how she saw Mother Mary holding Baby Jesus. Up to this time, she told me that she had never told anyone else. She always wanted to say to her daughters when they came to see her, but they would always start talking about something else.

I have never seen Buni cry before. Tonight, she cried right in front of me while telling me about her dream. We were both crying when she finished. It was the most beautiful story I have ever heard.

We continued talking, and she told me about her favorite passage in the Bible. It is Psalm 143. I will never forget that. I read it to her, and I still read it now, though she is no longer here. Then I read to her my favorite passage, 1 Corinthians 13:1. These two biblical passages remained the most inspiring texts of my life. It was the best night I have ever spent at home with my Buni.

May

Asma Nooruddin

Once the snow melted, my mother regularly arranged picnics for our family and friends. Our favorite spot was near the mountainous river of Kabul. It took about an hour to drive through the winding roads to get there. My mother would usually be at the wheel while my father accompanied her in the passenger seat. My mother was the more confident driver between the two of them.

On one occasion, we brought the Bangladeshi ambassador's daughter to our picnic spot. In the late spring, the rocky landscape by the water turned green with vegetation. We met some locals who came out to enjoy the scenery. They shared their freshly cooked rice and meat with us, and my mother gave them some of her delicious homemade cooking in return.

After we finished eating, the ambassador's daughter decided to wash her drinking glass in the pristine river. The moment she dipped her glass in the water, the current whisked it away from her hand. We cried out in shock. She was dumbfounded. She had no idea that the current would be so strong. After we got over the initial surprise, we all burst out into laughter.

We had a great fondness for the ambassador's daughter. Once, she invited us to a tea party on the lawn of the Bangladesh Embassy residence. As I played with my siblings on a grassy hill, she brought over an adorable children's tea set as a surprise gift for me. I was so touched by her thoughtful gesture. I cherished the tea set until it suddenly disappeared after our family moved to Bangladesh in '78. I have a sneaking suspicion that it was left behind in Afghanistan.

Looking back, I wondered what motivated my parents to take us to these picnics and playdates. When I asked, my mother told me that my father's work at the embassy frequently required her to attend several events and formal parties with him. She felt the constant socialization took away from the time they wanted to spend with us. Thus, she decided to share the weekends with her children in a more serene and natural setting.

The best thing you can spend on your children is time. Thanks to my mother's attentiveness, I never felt that my parents were too busy to play with us.

Elena

Dana Fodor Mateescu

Her name, I don't know, and I don't understand why. It seems to me, even today, that it's a song torn from the root, like an orchard full of ripe grapes hit by the storm.

"*Elena.*" When I say it, she does not come out of me but enters. You can't even hear it outside. It's a whisper, a breath. For me, "Elena" means white bat, strawberry, white cabbage stalk, Flodni, hazelnut, honey cake, the Danube loving the sea, fields with sunflower, dust, fields with ripe wheat, Borcea, sand, tuberose, and smiles.

When I say "Elena," it sounds like a cathedral. That is what my brain hears, not my ear. *It's her!* A name like a Gothic cathedral, it's a name that echoes in every other sound. A tall name that creates stone warheads. The "E" prepares you for "le-na," meaning "be careful, I am the solar, the bright, the bright."

A bunch of poppies grows in her heart. Water dripped from my Elena and a clay clock ticked. Her mistakes look for me and find me every time.

Elena was my mother, and she lived within me.

For you

Angelina Nădejde

I will surround the garden of your soul
with white roses,
wild
climbing,
so that no one might hurt you.

So you know that I am always there
near you,
from place to place, I will plant
a yellow one
to guard over
the white ones.

I will sprinkle them
with tears of joy
and I will plant between them
love.

I will ask the autumn of life
to keep them in bloom
forever.

If and only if
they would begin to lose their petals
out of sadness,
I will make a perfume
of them
and I'll call it
petals of the soul.

Adina

Silvia Grigore

A few years ago, the little girl who lived on the brink of subsistence worked, learned, and became a doctor. She grew up on a block with poor neighbors and two younger siblings with parents who quarreled all the time. The state-subsidized their heat for the winter, but they required proof of income every month. Because he could read and write, Viorel, Adina's father, was chosen by the people in the apartment building to be the administrator who took care of the distribution of consumption for each family.

At that time, I was a mayor's office clerk. It was my responsibility to gather and centralize all these files from the administrators of the social apartment buildings in the city. Every month Viorel's file was very well prepared. However, one day, he came into my office, drunk and quarreling, saying ugly words to me. I could not calm him down, and I had to call security.

After I calmed down, I wrote a complaint and sent an email to the department that deals with the training and pay of administrators.

Two days later, a beautiful but sad girl entered my office. Her eyes, big and gentle, were ready to burst into tears. She begged me not to fire her father because the family would have nothing to live on. She had two more siblings, and her mother was ill. I understood that she was the daughter of Viorel, the drunken and recalcitrant administrator. Although she was a minor, she did his work after she did her homework and helped her mother with chores. On top of all this, she earned a merit scholarship.

I looked at her and saw I had a force of nature in front of me—a child who had been beaten by fate but who was stubborn to overcome her condition honestly. I knew then that I would withdraw the complaint, which is precisely what I did. Time passed, and Adina learned and worked. I moved to another job.

After so many years, I am happy that Adina has succeeded! She told me that she finished high school and entered a school of medicine with a scholarship, and in the second year of college, she married a classmate. Adina became my doctor, and because of her, my life changed. God always sends you the people you need!

Prayer

Ana Maria Rosu

July 15, 2019

God is the sun and the moon
That goes to earth and heaven.

He is the whisperer of good,
He is the whisperer of wisdom.

He makes good choices,
So that we do not make bad choices.

He whispers to us from heaven
Good choices to us.

Team Building

Luminita-Elena Stoenescu

It was Saturday morning, and I was waiting with my colleagues for the bus to come to go to a team-building seminar in a cottage in the mountains. The company organizes such meetings to encourage us to get to know each other better and work better together to increase productivity. I was a department assistant and made all the necessary arrangements for the event.

I asked if I could take my pet, a Labrador, and the answer came in the affirmative from everyone. The bus arrived on time. My colleagues sat comfortably in their seats, but when I wanted to get on the bus, I was stopped by the driver, who told me that pets could not get on the bus. I told him that I had arranged everything, and I also called the contact person from the transport company, but he did not answer the phone.

The driver did not care, and my colleagues were impatient. The team coordinator came to see what the fuss was about and made a painful decision. He got on the bus and told the driver that they were all ready to leave. The bus started moving, and I was left on the sidewalk with the dog.

I felt a great pain in my heart. My colleagues abandoned me without trying to help me and without finding any solution. They just left. I started sauntering towards my house, but I followed a longer path as I wanted the effort to drive away from the pain, from my heart, and the indifference of my colleagues from my mind. I arrived home sad and tired. One of my colleagues called me to tell me that the person from the transport company eventually called the driver and said to him that he determined to go with the dog, but the bus had gone too far, and they did not return.

On Monday morning, when the director found out, he scolded everyone, telling them that the team building started right from the first moment of the morning, before the bus left and that everyone failed the test. My colleagues created a poster with their signatures and a photo of my Labrador and me to show their regrets. The poster said, "We all missed you in this team-building," and gave it to me. I hung the poster in the office. My Labrador stayed there for a long time in front of everyone.

Forced to Escape

David M. Oancea

The story I repeatedly heard until my father's passing to his eternal abode was a story from his late teenage years. It's the story of a young man who grew up in a village in Romania.

Life was hard but very full. He learned to be self-sufficient and was unafraid of tackling challenging tasks. He developed a rich culture where oral history, hard work, and close relationships were essential aspects of the fabric of daily life. If it had not been for political changes at the time and his friendship with a partisan, he would most likely not have ended up in the United States, and I wouldn't be telling this story.

Shortly after he turned 18, he had two choices: be arrested by the local police or leave the country. Although he anticipated the possibility of arrest ahead of time and had made plans, his decision to leave was spontaneous and unavoidable. As he repeatedly recounted throughout his life to anyone who would listen, the traumatic events of a Sunday afternoon and all the dangerous experiences that followed created an identity that defined him for the rest of his life.

My dad was a master storyteller. He told his story in such detail that I felt like I was there, reliving his experience. One of the best memories of my life was visiting Romania with him and hearing him retell the story in the place where it happened. Even when he began experiencing dementia, he would continue to tell his story as if he was reliving it again.

He viewed himself as an "overcomer." This identity served him well as he overcame one challenge after another to build a new life in a new world. His example of taking consistent and tenacious action without fear has been a gift to my brothers in our own lives and to me.

My own life has followed an unexpected and circuitous path. The courage, optimism, and unfailingly persistent attitude of my dad are the seeds that sprouted and have borne the best fruit in my life. These values in the face of any challenge, especially the one that forced my father to leave everything and everyone that he held dear behind, are the touchstones that continue to keep me grounded and forward moving.

A Cool Car

Eugen V. Rosu

For a car to turn heads, it must be of a certain brand. Perhaps the latest model or newest design is so different and unique that it stands out among the rest. Other cars can be decorated in such a way that they look like moving pieces of art. For others, it may be a convertible car with exciting passengers in it. Or the 90s cars with the giant speakers in the trunk that made everything shake when the music was blasting.

I drove none of those cars, and yet, people have turned their heads at my car. One day, in the Spring of 1991, it was late at night, around 3 a.m. I was returning from Easter service. In the rush of getting some older ladies in the car in a dark parking lot, I put a carton of red-colored eggs on the top of the car. I made sure everyone was safe. After they got all of their belongings in the car with them, I got in and left the church's parking lot. As I drove off, the egg carton slid down to the trunk.

While driving on Hollywood Boulevard in Los Angeles, I noticed the people on the sidewalk turning their heads after my car. I did not pay attention, nor did I stop the car to see if there was anything out of the ordinary. One by one, my passengers got out of the car, and finally, I got home. When I walked around the car, I saw the egg carton in the trunk. I showed it to my wife, and we both laughed at the fact that we drove on the highway and all over Hollywood Boulevard with the eggs all over the car. Then, we understood why the passersby turned their heads after our car.

Ah, you are probably curious to find out what car I was driving. It was a car that turned the heads of the passersby.

Life's Lesson

Silvia Grigore

I was in the car with my husband, and we were in a hurry. We were late for work. A group of children, also late, ran across the street through an illegal place in a curve. My husband pressed on the brakes.

For a moment, I was convinced that we had hit the little girl who was last in line. I couldn't control myself. I opened the car door and shouted, "Are you an idiot? Why aren't you being more careful?"

Immediately, her frightened look made me ashamed of yelling at her. "I didn't see. I thought I had time!" she said to me while trembling. My husband also shouted at her, "If we hadn't pulled the brakes in time, what would have happened? He restarted the car. I saw him look nervous. I knew we didn't have time for explanations, but the shock remained in my soul. I wish I could have gone down and hugged that scared little girl. She was just a child who made a mistake. How could I make it right? Why did I react like that?

Once I got to the office, I burst into tears. My work was off that day. Two weeks later, I went to that intersection around the same time, but the girl did not show up. I wanted to know if she was okay. After not seeing her for a while, I gave up.

More than a year later, I was invited as a writer to a children's literary club. I recognized the little girl among the club immediately.

She was confident and talented. I asked her if she knew me, and she didn't remember me. I reminded her of the incident on the street.

She said, "Ah yes! Now I remember."

"Do you remember what I told you then?"

"Your husband asked me what would have happened if he hadn't pulled the brakes in time, and then I was petrified. I could have died. I thought a lot about what he told me. "

So, in that crisis, that little girl turned into an angel. She had not heard or perhaps had not given importance to my inadequate words. She remembered only the words that had been a life lesson. She had realized the danger and had defended herself by living the joy of escaping with life. Since then, whenever I live in a complicated situation, I think about how I could help, not revolt.

Thank you, forgiving girl!

Surprised By Life

Silviana Carter

Elena is 28 years old and a student at the mathematics faculty, where her father pushed her to go. She wanted to enter acting school in Bucharest. After selling everything from her dormitory, she decided to prepare for acting. She managed to enter after five years.

At the age of 25, she went for the first time for the admission exam. The examining committee told her that she was old, had a muffled voice, and could not be heard in the tenth row by the spectators. At the age of 29, she entered with pretty good grades, which placed her 18th on the list out of 56 admitted candidates.

The first year was very hard. Her father gave her a few dollars a month. She received help from her college. She was happy to succeed in college, but she had nothing to eat. For a year, she ate just rice and became ill. She ate rice with milk in the morning, rice with salt at noon, and bread with rice in the evening, without knowing that it would hurt her.

The second year, she could not stand it anymore and ate fried or boiled potatoes in the morning, at noon, and in the evening, and it was better, but she was still generally hungry.

Elena knew that if she showed that she was hungry, being at an excellent college, she could be marginalized, especially since she had been told that no one cared about students' problems and that those who could not support themselves could leave.

Seeing her great desire to finish this college, a colleague helped her with a job in a video chat, and Elena, a naive person with no knowledge of English, accepted.

The first day was quite strange. She won only $150 because she did not understand what "Stand up pls" meant. She was asked to get up, but she thought 'standing' came from 'sitting,' and she was sitting and laughing.

After a year and a half at that job, she had enough money for food, but she felt very guilty in her soul. She contacted a priest and asked to confess. Her soul was heavy. She later met an American citizen and stopped working for the video chat. Her life changed, and her acting career took off.

Father's Letter

Mariana Alexandrescu

Every morning, I find a letter from Dad. I found the letter when I open the mailbox in my heart.

In front of the door, eagerly waiting, are war and worry. I can't tell them apart. They are so crowded that I confuse them. As I open the door each day, I rush. But they can't come in without my consent.

Somewhere, hidden by them, is a precious daily letter from Dad, waiting to remind me to open the Love in them. But no! Noisy worries demand my full attention. I look at them. They see it as an acceptance and rush in.

Today I managed to save the letter from under the hurried and barbaric feet of worry. I cried bitterly after I opened it.

"Beloved child," I extinguished the Moon and Stars and lit your Sun.

I also opened some popcorn for you in the morning. I colored them differently. I poured perfume on some of them. You can check. If you have time, pay attention to the carpet of leaves. In the trees, I sent you birds to hop and hop. Don't forget to look up. I put blue on you as far as the eye can see. Relax. I painted the leaves green, but I converted their colors to break the monotony during this period. What do you say? Soon, I will strip the plants and trees to make room for the snow with which I will cover them all. They will be fine under the duvet. I guarantee you. Don't be sad! I will raise them in the spring. Rest until then and wait with confidence. Have I ever let you down?

The world in which my first children, your most distant ancestors, chose to live is not your friend, but don't be afraid! I never left you.

I'm here.

Anytime, anywhere. I know everything before I am. I'll reach out to catch you.

If you cry, it's at the expense of future happiness. Nothing is in vain. If the road seems endless to you, and you get lost. If you hear my voice, get back on the safe path! I sent you my messengers and angels. I'm waiting for you tirelessly.

I love you.

FATHER

Be Considerate

Luminita-Elena Stoenescu

Early in the morning, in a small provincial town, a line of people stood in front of the bakery. The bakery smelled of warm, steaming bread. A young man parked his bicycle alongside the building and stood in line.

As he stood in line, he saw a man with two patrons in front of him take a handkerchief out of his pocket. As he did so, a 50-dollar bill fell out of his pocket. The young man was the only one who saw the banknote as everyone else was distracted by their discussions.

For a moment, he thought of stepping forward and pocketing the money. He considered putting his foot on the banknote and pulling it lightly towards him. He thought against the idea and quickly shook his head as if with the desire to throw his idea as far away from him as possible. Then, slightly agitated, he thought of shouting to the older man that the money had fallen out of his pocket, but he thought it would have disturbed the discussion of those in front of him. He decided against this idea as well.

The young man got out of line, picked up the banknote, and gently said to the old man, "This banknote fell out of your pocket the moment you took out your handkerchief." The man smiled at him, thanking the young man for his consideration.

On that sunny spring day, two happy people went to their homes. One man was comforted with the fact that there are good people in this big world, and one man chose selflessness. Honesty, delicacy, and care are noble qualities that honor us. The way we act and communicate says a lot about us. Not all thoughts that cross our minds are worthy of consideration. What matters are the thoughts that do not hurt those around us and the ones that make God smile?

Sleepwalking Candy Sales

David M. Oancea

"Would you like to buy some candy?" When I was on my first T-ball, around the age of eight or ten, the team held a fundraiser. Each player received a cardboard box with a handful of smaller boxes of peanut butter cups to sell to family, friends, and neighbors. I remember being excited to go out the next day and sell, so I took the box into my bedroom and set it next to the dresser.

The next morning, my mom told me that I had entered my parents' bedroom in the middle of the night with the box in my hand and had asked them if they would like to buy some candy. I had no recollection of doing that. Before this, I had experienced several instances of sleepwalking and sleep talking but could never remember anything the following morning.

Only recently have I learned more about the conscious and subconscious mind. The subconscious mind never sleeps. It governs all the vital processes of the body when awake and asleep. How important and powerful this aspect of our mind is! It's been compared to the earth in a garden—whatever is planted will grow, whether it's good for us or poisonous.

We have to be careful with what goes into our subconscious mind when the conscious mind is "off-duty." How many inventors, healers, and other problem-solvers have harnessed this mysterious aspect of our existence to make quantum-leap advances in all areas.

For me, this experience of attempting to sell candy while I was still sound asleep lifted the veil that normally covers the actions of the subconscious mind to show that it never sleeps and has amazing potential to accomplish our greatest dreams and desires.

Happiness

Anastasia Ciuntu

I want to be a happy person. I want to be what I am not. All people feel happiness, but no one has been able to measure or define it in a period. Happiness is given to us all in a measure that does not create dependence but allows us to rise from Hell.

What do we know about happiness? We all aspire to this abstract feeling, looking for something that will miraculously make our lives a fairy tale, where the world is painted in shades of pink.

What is unhappiness? This well-known feeling takes over our lives. Maybe because we dream too big in too small of a world. Maybe unhappiness happens when we run after the freedom promised in storybooks that our mothers used to read to us. We run in a vicious circle, searching for happiness. We choose to hurt ourselves to find happiness, to even suffer to finally receive a dose, which for an addict is not enough. It is never enough. We want more and more. We want to be what we are not.

Why do we seek happiness apart from all human experiences? We are deceived by the illusion of the idea that hides so many expectations through its sonic brightness. I want to feel happiness, but without even realizing it, when I hear this word, I think of my mother, my father, my best friend, and the person in the future who will be decisive.

Happiness is, in fact, our most precious desire. Something every soul seeks. *I am proud of you, Ana!* Will I hear that soon? Later?

I'm still waiting for my happiness.

Where Did She Go?

Ronald Rock

The wooden stairs leading to the backyard of the deck had shifted. The posts securing the risers had lifted. They needed to be reset, redrilled, and new lag bolts needed to be inserted.

My high school-aged daughter offered to run up to the hardware store and get them. She was in training for soccer and said the mile or so run there and back would be a good workout.

It was a hot and humid July afternoon. Not all the streets had sidewalks. She insisted she would be fine because she had run through the neighborhood numerous times before. We agreed on the specific route she would follow. I gave her cash, the lag bolt to match, and a kiss. Off she went.

Some time had gone by. I remember thinking she should have returned by now, even if she had walked part of the way. I got into the car, following the agreed-upon route to the hardware store. She was nowhere to be seen. I went up the back steps into the hardware store. To the left of the landing, there was a receipt, a lag bolt, and spare change.

But my daughter wasn't there, and the hardware store was closed!

I went into a deep rabbit hole, assuming that the worst-case scenario was happening. Shock, disbelief, confusion, denial, and intense guilt all consumed me. My stomach was in knots. I couldn't breathe. I felt paralyzed. How could I have failed her so miserably?

There must be an explanation. I retraced the route several times, hoping to see her sitting under a tree or resting. Nothing. I ventured off into a neighboring development, searching the streets. Nothing. I went home and called a few of her friends who lived along the route. Nothing. My anxiety and fear were crushing me.

Do I call the police? Do I call her mother? I decided to follow the route one more time. I prayed to God and St. Anthony for help.

Suddenly, my daughter was jogging off to the right as if nothing had happened. She had lag bolts in hand.

My immediate and overwhelming sense of relief was indescribable. I pulled into the next driveway calling her to get into the car.

She was finally safe in my car. My hugs and kisses took her by surprise. She looked confusingly into my tear-soaked eyes. I could finally breathe. I thanked God for answering my prayers.

Parenting Without Manual

Dana Fodor Mateescu

When Andrei was five years old, I took him to kindergarten. It did not last more than four weeks, and, even then, Andrei had broken. I tried enrolling him at several state and private institutions, but they failed to stick.

One day, I started playing with the kids in the classroom. I took off my shoes, and I rolled on the floor with the children in Andrei's class. I tickled them, got under the tables, and ran on all fours with them. I sang and yelled and played with them. "After me!" I would repeat all the movements. I would crouch, meow, and bark with them. And it was fun! I was in my world with the children.

The teacher was stunned. She had never seen such a fool in her life! But what did I care about how the teacher saw me when the children were not having a fun time? I loved playing with the kids!

This whole time, I noticed that Andrei was not playing. He was sitting in a corner, sighing at me. Then, I understood. He was jealous that I wasn't playing with him. *Nothing pleases this handsome boy!*

Half an hour later, after having fun with the kids, I told them I had to leave. The kids started buzzing around me. I did not expect that. The kids were crying for me to stay. I said goodbye and left the classroom, sweating profusely. I ran to the parking lot, where my husband was waiting for me.

Two days later, the teacher told me not to attend classes anymore because she couldn't do play with the kids in the way I did. I took Andrei for about three more days and then kept him at home. He was happy.

About a year later, I saw two of the children, twin brothers, from Andrei's old class. They were with their grandmother at a mall in Băneasa. When they passed me, they smiled at me and said, "Grandma, Grandma! Look! It's the woman who made us laugh in school!"

And I was happy that day.

The Wind of Change

Emilian-Ciprian Ene

About ten years ago, I was alone, and I thought no one could love me. I kept trying, and I saw that I couldn't. I was trying to meet someone, and I found nothing that connected. I went to the monasteries. When I arrived there, I prayed to see my partner. I was sick of searching.

At one point, I started talking with girls on Facebook. One of them replied to me. Through several conversations, she told me that she was an actress who said she could only work in Bucharest. At that time, I lived in Brașov. I considered her arrogant and thought she could undoubtedly do her job in Brașov. At that time, I had an awful opinion of Bucharest. I thought it was a very crowded city with dirty streets.

A few months passed, and my actress friend and I talked on the phone and on Facebook. We even got to meet in person. She invited me to Bucharest for a play performed by her improv class. There, I fell in love with the new city.

I made the best change for myself. It was the best decision to leave everything behind—friends, acquaintances, lovely places—to throw myself into the unknown and start life again.

My life has changed completely. I became a man who complains about the system, the bosses, and everything else. But, by being a small entrepreneur, I ended up doing coaching sessions with people who complain about everything in their lives. It was in this place that I could think better. I didn't think. I did what I felt and wanted. And it was good!

The Gift to Receive

Chris Dorris

I was at the very tail end of a remarkably emotional trip to Cabo San Lucas many years ago. I had created a lot of chaos for myself during that week. I had some particularly challenging personal life matters going on at the time. I debated on whether to even go on this trip, given what was going on in my world. Ultimately, I decided to go, and in retrospect, I am so immensely happy that I did.

The trip ended on a high note. I opted to extend it an extra day to do one of my favorite things in life, deep-sea fishing with just me and the crew. We caught so many fish that I ended the trip early because I could no longer use my arms anymore. After all, I was the only fisherman onboard. I was filled with joy.

I had paid for a full day of fishing but was perfectly content with the number of fish that we caught and assured the captain that I was beyond satisfied and we could cut the day short.

On the ride back to the marina, I reflected upon the long roller coaster of emotions of the week. The boat was traveling at full throttle, and we were nicely making a wake. There were perfect swells. It was the perfect boat ride and the perfect way to end my trip. Until I realized it just got even better. I looked to my left, and in the waves, our boat was being escorted by massive manta rays that were swimming alongside us. I couldn't believe my eyes. I had never seen such a thing. I grew up on boats. I have had many jobs on fishing boats. And I had never seen something so spectacular before.

I found myself weeping. Tears of absolute joy. Tears of absolute serenity. Tears come from a magical place of lightness of being. These magnificent creatures of the sea came to send me off with their love.

When we got back to the marina, I told the first mate that I didn't want any of the scrumptious tuna that we had caught. I told him he could have it all. And by the expression on his face, you would think I had given him a house. It was a magical moment. A perfect ending to a magical day. A perfect ending to a magical trip.

Easter Light During the Pandemic

Luminta-Elena Stoenescu

It is 2020. An unexpected pandemic has troubled people's hearts around the world. People could no longer attend the Holy Mass of the Resurrection because of restrictions, but I was one of the few who could attend. I volunteered to help the priest bring the Holy Light of Easter and the blessed bread to God-loving people who could not be present.

Authorities quarantined the city, and the streets were deserted. People were puzzled in their homes, listening to the alarming numbers of those severely infected shown on television. The father obtained the necessary documents to be able to circulate. The authorities stopped me, but they smiled and let me go when I showed them the volunteer badge and the data paper.

It was as if time stood still, and the streets were deserted, with no cars in front of me and none behind me. Everything seemed detached from another world, a world with tall buildings and deserted streets.

The Holy Liturgy of Easter was held after midnight, and it was a small number, no more than fingers of one hand. It was an uplifting moment that I lived and that I will remember all my life. I had a long list of phone numbers of people who wanted to receive the Holy Light. I felt a great emotion. I carefully carried the Easter Light in my hand, going to the addresses they told me on the phone. Between the blocks, I looked up and saw faces of people here and there, at the windows, waiting with a greater desire for the Easter Light and the blessed bread. They looked at me with joy as if I were an angel to them. People were coming down from their apartments, and I could only see their eyes escaping with joy with the masks covering most of our faces.

I greeted them and said fervently, "Christ is risen!" and they answered with tears in their eyes, "He is risen indeed!"

Their emotion was tremendous, and it affected me as well. I felt that I could have climbed the high mountains to see once again the joy in the eyes of the people, the fun of the Resurrection. One could feel the longing for God, and it was so obvious. Christ is risen!

Heroes

Eugen V. Rosu

We all like heroes. Some heroes have capes. Some heroes have only tight costumes and masks. Some heroes wear their underwear over the pants, but we understand because they need to leave in a hurry. Some heroes return from wars, and, unfortunately, some never do.

Then, some heroes practice a sport, and they end up being good at what they do. Not long ago, sports commentators were discussing a football player who managed to deliver a great number of precise passes. At the beginning of the game, the same sports commentators mentioned how much money the player was making, nothing outrageous. Only about 40 million!

Still, for me, there was a mystery. Someone is paid 40 million a year to pass a football and makes history by getting a record amount of passes. To tell you the truth, I am puzzled. How long will it take for a quarterback to get all the passes? I try and figure out how a man can be a hero. He is paid handsomely yet still misses some passes. Alternatively, I try to figure out how a car mechanic who is paid much less than a quarterback does his job. If he occasionally misses while fixing a car, it would not be good for the car owner. We would have to go back to riding horses.

What are heroes? Is your plumber a hero? If you are not sure, ponder this. What happens if the plumber misses a few "passes?" You don't want to step in that place, nor would you want to smell the air of that room. I know now that it is important to tip my daily heroes, though they may not look like the ones in the movies. They keep me going places and make my life function properly. Who is your hero?

Scars of Early Life

Silviana Carter

Ioana is a ten-year-old girl. Her biological parents gave her up for adoption when she was three years old, and her adoptive parents died in 2021. She wrote to me. After all, she did not trust anyone else to help her because she felt alone.

Last week, she was in my online classes, where we made up stories to express emotions, and she asked me to stay with her for a while after the course. The class had been about Pinocchio and his capacity for lying.

I confessed to the children that I also sometimes lie, even as an adult. I told them that you become stronger the more you tell the truth. Then, I told them that most lies are told not to upset others.

Ioana said, "I know that I lie almost all the time. I can't help myself, and I don't know what to do!"

"Okay, Ioana, but what you said now is a truth. You are brave to admit that you are lying!"

Surprised, Ioana answered, "Wow, yes, so can I tell the truth?"

"Yes!!!" I responded.

Then, when I was alone in the meeting, she told me she had jumped a fence, her mother was very upset with her, and her father slapped her on her cheek. He told her that if she did something to upset her mother again, she would fly out of that family.

I told her that I would take her if she were kicked out of the house. She said that another day, her father broke a hard-boiled egg on her forehead, and her head ached all night. I felt a terrible rage, like when my family beat me, but I had no one to tell. After the meeting, I decided to write a message to her mother to challenge her.

The next day, they withdrew her from my online center. I spoke to the one leading the group where her parents had come from, and she told me that Ioana was lying and there was nothing to do.

I left the group today, which supposedly provides emotional healing. I firmly believe that one can break the chain of child abuse even if you were raised in such a way. I decided to write the book 2 + 2 = 5 or *The Beating Of Children: The Beating Is Broken From Hell*.

I want to be able to prevent children from experiencing violence.

"Love Your Neighbor."

Chris Dorris

My father died at a very early age. He was in his forties, and I was nine at the time. And he was a very loved man with a lot of friends. He was full of celebration.

After he died, our family became less joy filled. Our house was suddenly more filled with fear and scarcity. We worried about how we would survive for lack of money.

My neighbors were Dan and Mame Kane. They had a daughter who they named Candy. As in Candy Cane. They were so full of joy and always celebrating. We lived at the Jersey Shore, in a town called Sea Isle City. My house was five houses from the beach, and the Canes were four houses from the beach.

I'd come back from the beach at 5 p.m. because that's when the lifeguards left. The Canes would be on their porch hosting some new family. They would have happy hour, ritualistically, on their front porch with cocktails and hors d'oeuvres. I would come over, stand on their lawn, say hello to everybody, grab shrimp, and listen to their jokes. I loved, loved, LOVED their vibe, and I would absorb the joy that they were bringing.

Eventually, my mom would scream, "Chris! Dinner!" and I would go home. Then, the Canes would retire inside for dinner. After dinner, they would move to their back patio, where they would celebrate all night with more cocktails and laughter.

I'd hear this laughter in my bedroom while I would try to read, but I couldn't focus because their joy and laughter were contagious. I would hear Mrs. Coffee, one of their guests, who had the loudest and most unapologetic laugh in the history of humans. I would find myself laughing, too, having no idea what we were laughing at but joining them in *the lightness of being*, and I intuitively knew that *that* is the best choice, *the choice to exist in lightheartedness.*

It was their constant decision to live in the lightness of being and celebration that inspired me to choose the path that I've chosen, which is to encourage people to choose the lightness of being. There is no coincidence that when you examine human peak performance, every person uses phrases like "it felt light" or "it just felt easy." There was no suffering, no struggle. *It felt effortless. It was fun.* There is great intelligence in choosing the lightness of being.

Thank you, Dan and Mame Kane!

A Woman Like Me

Martha Jijia

Our workgroup is diversified as far as age group is concerned. Within the group, there are two Millennials: one man and one woman. The man is calm and reserved. He is calculated in how he speaks and always dresses conservatively. The woman, on the other side, was different. Her skirts and dresses were so tight that she needed to pull them down constantly. When it came to accessories, nothing matched. Either the accessories were too small or too large. They were bold without saying anything. She had a few tattoos that could be detected through the sheer fabric high on her right arm. The one on her shoulder and above her left breast can only be seen with a lower shirt. How did she look? She is gorgeous!

One day after lunch, she made me a complimented that I looked suitable for my age. But her praise felt like a slight insult to my age. Truth be told, I am a few years older than her mother. As a result, I told her that I always looked good and intended to take care of myself for as long as I lived. Then, I told her that if she wanted to look as good as I look at my age, she might need to change her lifestyle. *Stop going to bars and drinking so much.*

On the other hand, I admired her. I saw her courage to face any challenge coming her way and never afraid to stand a fight.

The bar experience made her challenging. Later that evening, I pondered on "my age" and realized that I was a bit harsh on her, and perhaps it was difficult for me to accept my age. Or maybe I could see a bit of myself in the young woman, who reminded me of the Disco era. *Hmm, good times!* Each generation brings its flavor to society, and minor clashes are inevitable, but we do not need to make wars.

June

Asma Nooruddin

The thing I love most about Arizona is its genuine beauty. Within a single day, one can gaze upon the dignified saguaros of the Phoenix desert, stroll through the pine forests of the Sedona resort, and marvel at the stunning landscapes of the Grand Canyon.

Recently, my family made a weekend trip to Horseshoe Bend. It was breathtaking. The canyon's scale was far more remarkable in person than in all the postcards I had seen up until that point. We watched the sunset there, after which the wind picked up and sent loose sand flying into our faces. Luckily, I could use the tail ends of my headscarf to protect my eyes from the sharp particles. Through this incident, I realized why Bedouins always used to cover their faces. Their turbans were practical indeed.

To the north of Horseshoe Bend, just off the road, there is an unmarked site called The New Wave. I believe its name came from the cliffs which have eroded into gentle slopes. My youngest two and I decided to climb to the top, and I was pleased with how easy it was to walk along the natural staircase. Although my daughter brought her camera, our pictures could not fully capture the charm the area held.

We stopped by these locations on our way to Zion National Park in Utah, where I spent the entire day with my husband resting beside the riverbed. Our children went hiking together and returned in the evening to cool down in the water. It was such a calm and peaceful day. I felt nostalgic when I would picnic by the river in Afghanistan as a child.

I am glad my parents connected me to the natural world when I was growing up. I tried to continue this practice after I became a mother. In their earliest memories, my children recall picking berries in California. I wanted them to know the feeling of sunshine on their faces and the grass beneath their feet. By fostering the love of the outdoors in my children's youth, these trips have become a time for healing and reflection in their adulthood.

From the beginning of times, humans have always gone into nature to revive their spirituality. To find inner tranquility, a quiet space in the wilderness is the best place to be.

Happiness for Me

Angelina Nădejde

You may be wondering,
what is happiness for me?
It's the calm in which I can admire
the beauty of the flowering lilac,
from the garden of my house, on a clear
May morning.

My happiness,
a warm summer evening together with my friends,
listening to the soothing song of the crickets,
like an orchestra symphony.

My happiness, my children,
with the beauty of their youth, with their optimism,
and the worries they bring when they fall in love,
believing that this happens
just one time . . .

My happiness,
life next to my loved one,
the stolen kiss of a hurried morning

and the quiet moments of the afternoon,
without worrying about tomorrow because I know
I have a shoulder on which to lean.

My happiness, the beauty of the Sunday liturgy,
of the angelic singing of the chanters
and my connection with God through prayer.

That is my happiness!

Take an Extra Minute

Luminita-Elena Stoenescu

It was freezing cold this snowy winter. People were in a hurry to get to their warm homes as soon as possible. I was on my way to the hospital. I went there daily with goods for my poor mother, who had been hospitalized for a few weeks. The doctors were reserved. They didn't tell me when my mother would be able to go home.

One day, as I left the hospital after one of my regular visits, I noticed that the snow was particularly heavy. I felt the cold in my red cheeks as I hurried down the alley. I walked with my head bowed down and my chin nestled in my scarf.

At one point, I saw a card in the snow. I bent down to pick it up and saw that it was a person's health card. All sorts of thoughts were running through my mind. I thought of leaving the card there, but I could see that the snow would soon cover it.

I decided to take it to the hospital reception. I showed the card to the person at the information desk, but the lady told me that the card's owner was not in the database and, therefore, not hospitalized at the hospital.

What could I do at that point? I thought about the person who needed the card. I remembered that another hospital was nearby, so I brought the card there. I showed the card to the receptionist, and, this time, to my delight, I found out that the person in question was a patient at the hospital. I left the card with the nurse caring for the patient.

I felt great comfort in my heart and was proud of being able to do a good deed. I was happy to provide value to someone that day. Such gestures cannot be taken from us neither here nor in eternity. Good thoughts and deeds are our true treasures.

A Great Day

Ana Maria Rosu (9 years old)

I was walking in the park with my father, looking at the geese swimming in the pond. I wanted to find the right spot for fishing. I did not want to bother the geese, and I did not wish the geese to bother me.

Three boys were fishing there. Their grandfather helped them with the fishing rods. As I was about to cast my line in the pond, two older boys said I could not fish because I was a little girl. Then, they challenged me to a game of fishing. Their grandfather told them he needed to do more work on their fishing rods, but they would not listen.

We all put our lines in the water. Within seconds, I had a bite. I rolled back the line, and I got a fish. The boys were so upset and called my win beginner's luck. The grandfather told them that they should not challenge girls.

I was so full of joy, and I allowed the boys to take pictures with my fish. I told them that that was a good game. Their grandfather congratulated me on my success and gave me a high-five.

What a great day!

Life as it happens

Kay Huber

In the winter of 1966, I experienced the joy of giving birth to my first child, a baby girl. She was beautiful in every way. I was blessed to have my baby. I loved her so much.

By the time she was eight months old, it was apparent that she had some paralysis when trying to use her left hand and left foot. I took her to our family doctor. He called in a specialist, and they did some testing. They concluded that she had a stroke in the birth canal.

How this would affect her life was unclear. I took her to physical therapy, and we exercised at home. She was 14 months old when she was able to walk unaided. Getting around school, however, was a new challenge every day. In the morning, she would often fall getting onto the school bus, and in the afternoon, she would fall out of the school bus. Gym class was not her strong suit either. When she made up her mind to do something, that was the course of action she would take. She was tenacious.

She studied to be a social worker. The summer before her last semester in college, she came home to tell me she was expecting a baby. My thoughts rushed to her physical challenges. How could she take care of a baby? I am a Christian. I do not believe in abortion, but that is what I encouraged her to do. Several months later, she gave birth to her baby girl.

Her baby was precious and wonderful. My thoughts went to how could my daughter carry books and a baby? How could she feed a baby? How could she diaper a baby?

In December 1988, a car struck my daughter in front of the local post office as she crossed the road through a crosswalk. She died. She was 22 years old. My granddaughter was eight months old.

Today, I have a grown-up, beautiful granddaughter. She is married and has two young children. She lives close to my home. She and I love and encourage each other. I have been blessed.

From Psalm 81:16: 'With honey from the rock, I will satisfy you.'

Above All, We Must Pray!

Cornel Todeasa

"Prayer is a conversation with God," said St. Gregory of Nyssa. St. John Chrysostom echoed this when he wrote, "We truly speak with God at the time of prayer."

God responds to our prayers. He enters a dialog with us. This is the promise the Lord made when He said, "Truly, I say unto you, if you ask anything of the Father, He will give it to you in my name . . . ask, and you will receive that your joy may be full," (John 16:23-24).

It is understood that there are two kinds of prayer: private and corporate. However, this view is erroneous, for it falsely divides prayer. The "right belief" is that prayer has wings, and both are needed for flying to heaven.

There is the prayer during which we talk privately to God. The Lord says, " . . . when you pray, go into your room and shut the door and pray to your Father Who is in secret, and your Father Who sees in secret will reward you" (Matthew 5:6).

There is also the corporate prayer that we offer to God in a chorus. "How lovely is your tabernacle, O Lord of Hosts . . . My heart and my flesh cry out for the living God . . . Blessed are those who dwell in your house. They will still be praising you" (Psalm 84:1-4).

Some insist corporate prayer is the most important. This is based on the fact that the Lord prayed together with his disciples and told them, "Whenever two or more are gathered together in my name, I will be in the midst of them" (Matthew 18:20).

Truthfully, both types of prayer are important and should be integrated into one prayer. One without the other is not complete and, thus, not sufficient in our spiritual journey. It is important to both pray privately in our homes as well as in the House of God, His Church, His people, and His angels.

The perfect example of complete prayer is given by our Lord Himself, who not only prayed alone in solitary places but also with His disciples, the people in the temple, and elsewhere.

Approach God with one prayer that has two sides, for both are equally important for our salvation. St. John Chrysostom said, "What water and sun are to the body, prayer is to the soul." This reminds us that no matter where we are, in private or in public, above all, we must pray.

Needs

Em Sava

In the house across the street from my own home lived an Indian family. I do not know how big the family was. I often saw chairs and legs of people dressed in traditional white costumes through the garage door. I unwittingly thought of Preda's Iocan's Glade and marveled at the cultural Babylon of North America and its social permissiveness.

People sat in a semi-darkness created by the windowless space, lit by a dim light. Sometimes, I saw an older man coming out and setting fire in the garage. I marveled again at the kindness of the neighbors who accepted their habit and did not call the police and firefighters. In time, they understood that the man was caring, and they were not in any danger.

Sometimes, I saw a woman with a newborn, a grandmother with a lovely earring on her forehead, and two kindergarten children: a girl of about four years and a boy of about six. The little boy was more daring, and, one day, he talked to me and said, "sisteeeee," as he pointed to the girl. Then, he told me that they came to Canada because there was snow there, and they could make snowmen. The little girl smiled wryly, not daring to say anything.

Another day, I fractured my leg and started wearing ice like a fairy tale. The Indian grandmother came to me with a kind of glue and insisted on putting it on my leg. Even though I did not put it on and did not believe in Indian folk remedies, I greatly appreciated the kindness and desire to help me. I told her she had a beautiful earring, and she laughed, tickled like a teenager, happy at the compliment.

People are good. All over the world, there is a meadow of Iocan, sometimes in a garage on a Canadian street.

Don

Luminita-Elena Stoenescu

As a child, I lived surrounded by animals of all kinds. From experience, I realized that animals communicate with humans. While they do so very delicately, their messages are often clear, caring, and loving.

Don the Labrador was playful and friendly. These are characteristic of all Labradors. Labradors are not guard-dogs, and they love the company of people of all ages. To my husband and me, Don was the most intelligent and cutest pet in the world. Moreover, Don managed to soften our reactions and lighten our moods.

When Don was with us, we lived in an apartment in the middle of the city. When my husband and I went to work, Don sat alone in the apartment, waiting patiently yet eagerly for us to go out to the park together on our return. On busy days at work, if I didn't get home at the usual time, the wait became longer for Don.

Once when I finally got home, Don was calm, much too calm. At first, I thought maybe he had done some damage to the house. Perhaps, he had bitten a slipper or shoe, so I searched around, but I didn't find anything out of order. I went to change his water. Because he could not hold it in any longer, Don urinated in the container from which he drank water.

Why do animals make such decisions? I do not know the answer to this question. Sometimes, when my husband and I argue, Don will disappear from the room and go roll around in the bathtub. It was as if he was trying to grab our attention to notice the absurdity of what he was doing so we would stop arguing.

Actions like this exceed our expectations of what pets are capable of showing. Don was sending us a message. I firmly believe that animals can respond to people's love. Many years have passed since Don is no longer with us, but I often remember the special connection created between us that will never disappear from my heart and mind.

My New Dress

Dana Fodor Mateescu

When I was three, my father and I took my grandmother to the train station. While there, I ate a donut. I jumped around on one leg and sang, "cuckoo-cuckoo!" I was happy and laughing up to my ears.

Being with my father was a delight. He let me do almost anything. He let me take off my shoes on the train, perch on the couches, stick my head out the window, spits, and scream.

On that day, it was raining. I wore a dress. I can remember my father shouting to me, "Calm down! You're going to fall into that puddle!"

It didn't end well.

Bam! I fell onto the ground into a puddle full of mud. I had dirt on my face and in my mouth. My doughnut rolled away. The dress was filthy. My knees were bloody and full of dirt.

I started screaming in pain. My father shouted, "See what happens when you don't listen? Why don't you listen to me?"

He wiped me with what he could, took off my dirty dress, took me by the arm, and brought me to the Sora store. I was just in panties and sandals and dirty as hell. I didn't even look like a girl anymore. Everyone looked at us like a bear just walked into the store. I hummed slowly, with some guilt, but I was so happy because my father didn't scold me further. The saleswoman, acting motherly, wiped me with a wet cloth. She washed my face with cold water, made my hair cuter, and made me smile. "She is so cute. She looks like a little boy!" she said.

The whole thing was over.

He bought me a dress from Sora. The dress was blue, stretchy, and smelled of newness. I loved it like a friend because it was from my father.

Funny Crepes

Emilian-Ciprian Ene

I worked with crepes. I made crepes on the street for four years, developed them, and saw what worked and what didn't. I created new tastes and named them. I named my business Funny Crepes.

The name came to me when I was selling them at a subway station. We noticed that people were sad, and I found that the name could change their mood a little. I thought that this name would be best for my crepes.

From here, I managed to make myself known in the area and became appreciated by people who thought that crepe-making was not an easy job to do. At one point, I received an invitation to give an interview to a national newspaper. I was open to that, which made me and my crepe business more well-known. Then, I received an invitation to a TV show on a national station. This appearance made me even better known. I also received orders and felt that I was getting closer and closer to opening a food truck with my crepes. I was so determined to get to the next part, and I hoped it would be my big opening, my big business.

The days passed, and the months passed. I had talked to a close acquaintance to see locations for my business. I kept searching for places and talking about my business, but nothing more. I was still there, and I couldn't take a step forward. I became frustrated, and my street sales were falling.

And then, one day, it happened. Together with another guy, I managed to open a food truck for my crepes.

If someone were to tell me 10-15 years ago that I would succeed in opening my own business, I would not have believed it. Now I know that your dream comes true when you want something from the bottom of your heart and have patience.

I know that when the time comes, I will start, and I will succeed.

What Am I Doing Here?

Mariana Alexandrescu

The first city in history was a failed attempt. God did not approve the request. Deeply wounded and saddened, he pointed dramatically, firmly, unequivocally, NOT to the city, but the crowds, to the living in overlapping layers! A vast Earth, adorned by the Divine hand itself, was the gift of heaven for man.

The enemy of flight is life in the gold box. Isolation puts the spotlight on this exact sequence, shooting the freedom-hungry mind with the question, "What am I doing here?"

I lived in the country until my third child was nine. My ex-husband decided to move to the city. My first impression was that the people in the building seemed cruel. Several children were kicking a deflated ball at the wall. But they didn't realize the lack. They were happy.

I froze for a few seconds, and then I mourned with so much pain that I felt like a mountain stone at the bottom of a precipice! My children were going to live there in a concrete box, identifiable as a number on a door, among many others.

The effect of this urban lifestyle was the dismemberment of my family.

My children had developed a particular sensitivity during the years of freedom lived in the vast space of nature. Their playmates were the snails out for a walk after the rain, which they lined up all over the yard, the birds rummaging through the hollows of the trees temporarily "seized" in the house, the wildflowers in the field, the trees adorned with buds, leaves, flowers, fruits, the unseen happiness of the earth, air, water, sun and moon, the scent of the wind, the rains and the joy of the sunrise and sunset.

They were friends with the forest and river, with the massive green meadows, with the crickets and frogs, with the abandoned kittens and puppies that slept with us in bed. The ample space that received their longing to fly also rejuvenated with the buds of life running through them tirelessly.

When we talk about their childhood, they don't remember anything about the gray concrete life. The first image that comes to mind from their green childhood is that of winter evenings, and they float, tumultuous and melted with happiness among the snowflakes and in the house waiting for them with hot stoves and hot tea.

This is the gift that they will always carry in their hearts, the stone they will place in all the corners of their lives.

A Corner of Paradise

Eugen V. Rosu

There was a special place where I enjoyed relaxing, reading, and dreaming of a child whose universe was the open sky, the horizons that held forests, and endless lands of wheat, corn, and vineyards. There was an apple tree in the middle of the vineyard. The tree had a branch that looked like the arm of a giant, where two branches split, forming a "Y."

At that point, I placed a pillow to rest my head while holding a book in my hand and immersed myself in the wonders offered by the writer. Young vines climbed through the tree's branches and somehow provided shade. Through the top branches, I could see beautiful clear skies and birds flying around, chirping with each other. There, I had my dog with me. It was relaxing at the bottom of the tree. On top of a branch near mine, there was my favorite cat.

The bees provided background music and flew above the trees. Their hives were about ten yards away from the tree, and I could hear the flying to and from the hive. Their work had a sweet taste and the fragrance of many flowers. My father took me with him to check on the bees. I was a little scared because I was stung by a bee before. My father prepared me and taped my clothes so that no bees could enter.

I was able to see a queen for just a few seconds. It was amazing to see the speed with which the queen and her guards moved around to avoid any threats. I saw the racks of honey filled with the sweet liquid dripping in the hive. The bees were the messengers between the alfalfa fields and my jar of honey. They brought the perfumed pollen from the linden trees to make that light, delicious honey. I saw the cleaner crew, which pushed outside the dead bees or anything that did not belong in the hive.

I could enjoy that deliciously sweet gift from my friends, the bees, every day. In the hot afternoons, I took refuge in the apple tree, enjoying the lecture of a book with the music provided by the bees. They were flying freely with no control tower, no traffic signs, and no accidents.

July

Asma Nooruddin

At long last, after leaving Afghanistan, I was reunited with my relatives in Bangladesh. Every day felt like a celebration, but the biggest celebration of all was the sacred month of Ramadan. During Ramadan, which was the ninth month of the lunar year, every Muslim would fast from dawn until dusk. The purpose of the fast was to take the attention we placed on our physical appetites and focus on nourishing our spiritual needs instead.

Once the sun set below the horizon, they would break their fasts with a meal called *iftar*. Even though we were usually not fasting alongside the adults, we could not wait for *iftar* since there would always be a feast laid out for us in the evening. We had a strategy to savor it properly. We would sample a little bit of each dish until we found our favorite, which we would save as our very last morsel.

At the end of Ramadan, we would celebrate Eid al Fitr, the Festival of Charity. The fast was officially over! Our parents would give charity to the poor and buy us colorful new clothing. After the Eid prayer, we gathered with our family and friends.

Two lunar months later, Eid al Adha, the Festival of Sacrifice, took place to celebrate the end of Hajj, the annual pilgrimage to Mecca. The rites of Hajj commemorate the actions of Prophet

Abraham and his family. God commanded Prophet Abraham to sacrifice the thing that was dearest to his heart, which happened to be his son. When Prophet Abraham and his son both submitted to the divine decree, God spared the son's life and told Prophet Abraham to sacrifice a ram instead. Therefore, Muslims around the world sacrifice livestock during Eid al Adha to distribute the meat to charity.

Every Eid, my maternal grandmother would invite the extended family to her home. On her property, there were several giant mango trees. We children decided to climb one of them. All of us perched on the branches like monkeys. Once, a thick branch my cousin was hanging onto broke off the tree. She tumbled to the ground and hit her head. Fortunately, she recovered, but we had learned our lesson. We stopped acting like monkeys from then on. I think we were just grateful to be together during these happy days, alive and healthy.

A Place to Wander

Mara Viliga

Today's thought takes me to a beautiful and quiet village in Crişana, a picturesque place in Western Romania.

We live in a century of speed, busy people, and busy schedules. We townspeople, who spend all day running against the clock and often feeling agitated, like to escape to nature, away from the hustle and bustle of the city. We enter the silence of the village to cross the quiet streets, where on summer mornings, you hear nothing other than the song of crickets. You can smell the fresh grass and see butterflies and birds flying.

In such a setting, it seems as if you are completely disconnected from the hustle and bustle of the city, and you are charged with the energy given by nature. You admire the view in front of you. A beautiful and quiet village that stretches along the road, the houses standing on either side and, behind them, rise towering green hills with their dense forests where you have the opportunity to meet a deer.

How comforting such a quiet area can be, with the fresh summer air and the chirping of birds charging you with energy, a wonderful place that seems to stop time.

It is summer, and the sun warms us with its intense rays. The plants stretch out, towering in the sun, giving us a beautiful landscape. Summer is the season of holidays, sunglasses, and long, hot summer days.

How beautiful everything is to make time to stop to admire nature, enjoying everything it has to offer.

The great Romanian philosopher Lucian Blaga rightly said that eternity was born in the village. Once you reach this corner of heaven, on the border of Crisana and Banat, time seems to stand still. The speed and noise of the city here remain just a memory. It is the perfect place to meditate in peace and find your lost balance.

Inspiration

Brenda Whillock

As a parent, I question myself daily about the decisions and choices I have made in my life. The pressure of always trying to do the right thing and be the best example for our kids, yet being human, we often fall short. When I stop and look back at the choices and decisions my children have made, it makes me realize maybe I did not need to worry and stress so much. My children have somehow picked up on my best attributes and applied them in their everyday lives while seeing my shortcomings and working toward not repeating them. I am blessed to see them each come into their own persons with their own attributes and shortcomings, some familiar to me, and some they have all on their own.

A particular story of kindness comes from my younger son. He has always had a tender heart; all of my children do, but this particular one wears it much more outwardly than the others. He was playing in a basketball game in the 6th grade. One of his teammates had a deformed hand. That did not stop this kid's ability to give 100 percent and play to his best abilities. The game was a close one, and as the clock was running down and time was running out, we looked down the court for the play to happen, but my son was nowhere in sight. As all eyes were looking for the game-winning play, he was in the backcourt tying his teammate's shoe that had come untied. It was his teammate with the deformed hand who could not tie his own shoe quick enough during the game. I am not here to tell you if we won the game or not; to be honest, I do not remember, and I am quite sure my son would not remember either. What will never leave my memory is the kindness my son showed to another teammate and human. There are so many life lessons we all are privy to every day. We can choose to either sit on the sidelines and do nothing or go out of our way to show an act of kindness and human compassion for one another. These simple acts build our character for a lifetime. We have a responsibility to lead by example and do the right thing. We never know who is watching and how it will reach out beyond that moment.

"Again and Again, in Peace, Let us Pray to the Lord!"

Cornel Todeasa

With these words from the Divine Liturgy, we hear the priest asking us, the faithful, to join him in prayer. He is encouraging us not simply to join in prayer but in an "again and again" prayer, a prayer which is either a repeated one, an uninterrupted prayer, or both. He is asking us, as I understand the meaning of the repeated word again, to join him in persistent and fervent prayer.

This persistence in prayer brings to my mind the widow from The Parable of the Widow and the Judge (Luke 18:1-8). In this parable, the widow kept asking a corrupt judge to help her, again and again, until the judge said, "Even though I don't fear God or respect man, yet because of all the trouble this widow is giving me, I will see to it that she gets her rights. If I don't, she will keep on coming and finally wear me out!"

So, we have to pray and be in a dialog with our loving God again and again as long as we live. There are many dangers to our salvation around us. As we grow and journey through this life, we face again and again these dangers and temptations, so we must pray again and again. We must ask for God's help and guidance every day of our lives. For God will "judge in favor of His own people who cry to Him day and night."

Our prayer is not one prayer for the whole of life, but many ardent prayers for every moment of our lives.

The Fathers of the Church also encourage us to pray always. They gave us the "Prayer of the Heart" or the "Jesus Prayer" to pray again and again, unceasingly from the heart. "Lord Jesus Christ, Son of God, have mercy on me, a sinner." We should learn this prayer, keep it close to our hearts, and say it again and again. We can say this prayer silently everywhere and any time, while we are doing other things and when we are doing nothing. If we do this, we will never waste time.

Let us talk to God in prayer and cry to Him for anything. But above all, as St. Paul said, we should "in everything give thanks," again and again.

A Delayed Gift

Luminita-Elena Stoenescu

My husband and I spent nine years alone until the house resounded with the merry laughter of children. Nine years without children but surrounded by God's children. Looking back, I can see God's blessing and His care for us.

Our parents, who were wise people, received us with great love when we visited them in the house where we grew up. They were not insistent and were not disturbed by the fact that we, their children, did not have our own children.

The years flew by, and we often wondered why children did not come into our lives. Weren't we ready to become parents? We searched for answers to these questions. We did the tests required by the doctor, but the test results did not provide us with answers. From an anatomical point of view, there were no obstacles. We asked ourselves questions, but even this did not bring us into deep sadness. Many times, humans worry too much and put too little into work, so I decided to get directly involved in some children's lives.

I often went to the Children's Hospital, spending time with them and showing them affection. My husband visited children with cancer at the oncology hospital. We were like big children surrounded by children, but the desire to have children did not leave us.

We have never been met with insensitive questions or reactions from people on this subject. There is an expression with a lot of truth: "Who resembles, gathers." The people around us were also kind.

After nine years, we made an important decision. We thought to invite a stork to come to us. We adopted a five-year-old girl who had been abandoned three separate times. The biological mother had left her in the hospital immediately after her birth. The nursing nurse an adoption. A family kept her for three months, but they left her after three months. So, she joined our family. After we adopted her, it was as if God was bringing us next to other people who made the same gesture. Moreover, close friends adopted three boys, two brothers, and a little boy with motor concerns.

Two years after adoption, I gave birth to a baby boy. Now, the house is full of children's laughter.

Enchanted

Elena Lupu

The city was talking to her. It spoke to her through every tile on the pavement and through every glance of the locals who sat at the small tables hidden in the shadows of older buildings than they would have shown. She had dreamed of being there since she was little. But that had not prepared her for the reality she was living then. The present has this gift to make you feel everything deeper. It takes you by surprise with the simplest thing in existence: the state of being. And she was there. It was so much there that it was as if she could see herself in that light for the first time.

Not only was that city alive in a way that she could only feel, but it was also making her alive in a whole new way. She felt more and more changing herself with each step she took. And she had already taken many steps that day.

New places, new experiences, and new people can get out of each just as much as they are allowed. Prague already had a special place in her heart, but it would have had a special place in her development since then. The mere visit had aroused her curiosity, which she did not know she had. It had given her hope that she didn't even think could exist for her. And that's not because something extraordinary would have happened, in terms of standard expectations, but just because of how it made her feel inside. It made her feel inspired and full of life. And when does man have more desire to live than when he feels full of energy? Of emotion?

The visit had lasted only a day. But to plant the seed of a thought and an experience, one does not need more. It might even be too much. We are always looking for explanations for every little thing in life. Still, sometimes it is not necessarily about finding the ideal formula, but about being open and letting things unfold … to follow the way it develops and to act according to the present of that path.

Just for You

Angelina Nădejde

A rain of tears, I saw
Dripping,
from the sky of your eyes
and I thought
of the storm in your soul.

The thought that I'm your thunder
and lightning makes me sad.
I want to be your rainbow
of hope, love, and longing.

To be your sunrise every morning
when you look at me and your path to joy.
In the evening, to be the sunset over the day's troubles,
and at night, a guardian angel over
your dreams.

Moved to Tears

Ronald Rock

Have you ever heard music but been unable to pinpoint where it's coming from? Have you ever heard a tune that was unlike any song you had ever heard before? Have you ever listened to music that caused you to pause, take notice, and that moved you to tears?

For years, every day at noon, our hospital provided an opportunity for anyone to watch and listen to quality performances by local musicians, ensembles, and performing art organizations. For years, I had frequently heard the performances, but I was always too busy to stop and enjoy them.

On one of those busy days, I exited the elevator onto a walkway of the large three-story atrium overlooking the ground floor. Preoccupied, as usual, I heard the music mostly as background music. As it played this time, however, I was captivated by it. I froze and listened to it. I was completely immersed and mesmerized by the sound. It was pure and heavenly. It surrounded me as it magnificently echoed throughout the atrium.

As if by an unseen force, I was drawn by the music to the railing. Below, a musician was effortlessly playing her harp. A small crowd had gathered around her, absorbed by the enchanting notes. I closed my eyes, and what happened, I can't explain. The more I listened, the more divine the music became as if I became one with the music. Every note reached deeper into my being, into my soul. Deep emotions began stirring emotions I didn't know existed, emotions that brought tears to my eyes.

Once the melody stopped, I heard myself gasping for breath. For those few minutes, I found myself in what must have been heaven. Never has music so moved me. Had I not stopped that day, I would have missed one of the most inspirational moments of my life.

A Son's Love

Luminita-Elena Stoenescu

During World War II, a twenty-five-year-old man walked into the first floor of a building in Berlin. He had learned of his mother's condition and was on his way to care for her.

The situation outside was worrying. The gunshots were loud. Plane raids passed from time to time over the building. Everything outside was sad and gray. The son sat on the edge of the bed holding his mother's hand. He did not want to leave her alone.

Suddenly, there was the sound of a siren predicting misfortune and urging all the people to go down to the bunkers in the basement of the buildings. The neighbors ran as fast as they could down the stairs. Children cried. Everyone's heart was pounding.

The mother worriedly said to her son, "Go, my son! I can't come with you. I'm too heavy for you to carry me. Go, and live for me!" With tears in his eyes, the son said to his mother, "No, mother! Either we die together, or we live together!" And he dropped to his knees beside his mother's bed, holding her hand tight with his head bowed over her to protect her.

The bombing began in Berlin. Everything was falling, and the buildings crumbled like sandcastles. The son and mother kept praying in their minds and hearts. The son did not lift his head from his mother's body.

Suddenly, the bombing stopped. There was a great silence. You could hear the wind. The mother opened her eyes, and the son raised his head. They were both alive. Everything else around them, however, was destroyed.

Soldiers slowly took to the streets to see if they were survivors among the ruins of the buildings. They spotted the mother and son on the first floor of the flats. They were seated on the bed next to each other, with everything around them destroyed due to the bombing. All that was left was a bed with two survivors. Their love overcame death. God protected that place by seeing the beautiful, sacrificial love in their hearts.

My Ancestry

Dana Fodor Mateescu

I carry with me all the people I come from: the good, bad, beautiful, intelligent, ironic, brilliant, worthy, clean, stinky, lying, late, crazy, or stupid with the foam of the Black Sea. I hold a little of each within me. My roots are deep like giant snakes. They move under my feet from one end of the country to the other.

My father is Hungarian. My mother is a Bulgarian. For half a century, the eyes of my ancestors, blue and brown, have been with me. I feel them everywhere. But because I always did things differently, I didn't want to be like anyone. My eyes never turned brown to black. My eyes never took the look of a bitter child with shoes cut at the toes because they were too small.

I carry their freckles on my shoulders, and I hear their silences, worries, and strength. Their smiles all crowded into me. Their veins swell in my flesh, and their blood beats in my veins. I step on their bones with boldness and confidence.

I follow anonymous Jews, suiciders, and miners, smelling heavily of cheap brandy and death—my grandparents and soldiers with blood on their uniforms and decorations on their chests. My family's peasants gathered the wheat of others and drove ribs into horses. They witnessed hungry and amazed children who held dirty apricots in their mouths at the mouth of the Danube River.

They are all drawn on my face, in my history, as if someone left me a thousand faces with a thousand souls and a thousand lights. I have moments when I look like each of them and days when I am none of them, but I am their child, a child with a thousand parents.

Sticking to Principles: To Play or Not to Play?

David M. Oancea

During my childhood and throughout my teenage years, our family attended church services on Sunday mornings. My mom had taught us to say our daily prayers from an early age, and going to church was expected, one of those non-negotiable events of each week.

The church was a place to be present in a sacred space, to pray and learn with the community of believers, to serve others without expecting anything in return, to socialize with people that we didn't interact with the rest of the week, and especially to make time to thank God for all of his blessings.

As I came to the end of high school, even though I was extremely busy with schoolwork, school clubs, and organizations, my religious faith occupied the core of who I was. I also loved playing tennis competitively. Tennis and my other accomplishments as an athlete ranked high in my priorities.

The annual city tennis tournament in our small town brought out the best players. I had a good tournament and reached the men's singles final, where I was set to play a legend who I had looked up to ever since I started playing. There was one problem: the tournament director scheduled the final for Sunday morning, and he would not modify the schedule so that I could attend church services. I told him that I would have to forfeit the match since that was the only time services were held.

So, I went to church with my family. On our way home, we drove past the high school tennis courts and found out that heavy rain had postponed the match, which was now scheduled to be played in the afternoon when the courts would be dry enough. It was hard for me to believe, but I was pleasantly excited to be able to compete!

The match was a close three-setter. My high school coach was the umpire. I defeated my mentor for the first time, and I was overjoyed! The win was a spectacular confidence booster. More importantly, it taught me to do what I believe is right for me, to accept the consequences, and to move forward without bitterness or regret.

Love Conquers All

Stamatula P. Kretsedemas

The year was 1971, and I had been in the United States for seven years. A class was offered for foreigners who were ready to be naturalized in a nearby town. It was a four-hour class every Saturday, and to get there it was a 30-minute drive. My husband drove a friend and me there and back. I am from Greece, and my friend is from Germany. This lasted for several months.

As I was learning the basics of the constitution, I also improved my language with the help of the English dictionary.

At the end of the class, I took the verbal test at the immigration and naturalization office, which I passed. Then, we had an official ceremony in front of the whole high school body with the state governor in attendance as well as some local dignitaries. The purpose was to impress upon the students the significance of becoming an American citizen. It is something that should not be taken for granted.

Fourteen of us pledged allegiance to our new country. It was an emotional and proud day in my life, especially for one who came at the age of 19 with no prior knowledge of the English language.

Clear Sky

Chris Dorris

It was internship season during the second year of my master's program at Arizona State University. I had already worked as a clinical social worker in Atlantic City. Now, I was studying to be a sports psychologist working with pro golfers because golf was my new passion.

One day I was complaining to Theresa, a brilliant classmate of mine, that I didn't want another counseling job as an internship because I had already done that in Atlantic City. She let me vent for 3 minutes before she interrupted with two questions.

The first question was, "What would perfect look like?"

I said, "Well, I guess, in an unrealistic world, perfect would be to work with the men's golf team here at ASU, but what would they want with me? They're already number one in the world!"

She responded with a brilliant question. "Why don't you just ask?"

I thought, "You obviously don't know Division 1 sports. They're the best team. They're amazing. Why would they want me?"

But she did ask a very good question. Up to this point, I would not have asked because I would not have even entertained the possibility that the best-case scenario was available to me. But now, if I didn't ask, I'd be a coward. So, I decided to ask.

I went to my supervisor and asked if an internship for the golf team would count for my degree, and the answer was yes, but I needed a licensed psychologist who had experience with applied psychology as my supervisor.

Then, I went and asked the golf coach, and he said, "Sounds good; start with the freshmen, and if all goes well, you can work with the whole team!" Then, I went to the clinical site department to help find a supervisor, and they said, "The perfect guy for you is right across the hall, Dr. Linder!"

Dr. Linder said, "Oh my god! This would be so great! I'll teach you everything I know. Let's get started!!" He was more excited than I.

POOF! I created my perfect internship. I did so well, and it became a paid position after I graduated for ten years. Golfers from everywhere came to Arizona State University, and many became my clients as they graduated and went on to the PGA tour. Two questions propelled me from no experience to working with professional golfers.

Fear Not Death

Cornel Todeasa

"Death belongs to life as birth does," writes the poet Tagore. "The walk is in the raising of the foot as in the laying of it down."

St. John of the Ladder encouraged us to think about death. "As of all foods, bread is the most essential, so the thought of death is the most necessary of all work ... It is impossible to spend the present day devoutly unless we regard it as the last of our life."

My old grandfather Gavrila often said, "I already sent my application upstairs; when God approves it, I will go." As a child then, I was very impressed with his courage. But when he was sick and realized that his time was up, my brave hero prayed with tears, "I just want to live to see the daylight; nothing else do I want from life." He did not want to die.

My grandfather would have looked quite foolish in the eyes of St. Ambrose of Milan, who said, "The foolish are afraid of death as the greatest of evils, but the wise men seek it as a rest after their toils and as the end of evils."

Very few of us would be so wise in the face of death because we, like my grandfather, do not want under any circumstances to die. We are afraid of death.

One way – a very poor way – that we cope with the reality and the fear of death is to avoid thinking about it until we have reached old age and we feel the "time" for death is closer. If we postpone it now, it is likely that we will postpone it then and end up never dealing with the inevitability of our mortality. Moreover, we do not know the time when we shall be called.

So, how do we prepare for our death? Obviously, being "strengthened with the remembrance of death" (St. Barsanuphius of Gaza), we prepare daily by living an authentic Christian life, observing God's commandments. If, during our life journey, we walk on "the path that is straight and sorrowful and labor in silence" (St. Ephraim the Syrian), we will have no fear of death and our imminent judgment.

The Happy Bubble

Purvi Desai

We live in a world where our surroundings don't allow us to realize who we are and what we want fully, yet we all have one common need: the need to be happy. Very few of us understand that happiness is a state of mind.

I am a mother of two young children, and with all the sadness in the world, I worry for their well-being.

It is challenging to control the use of technology when we are so dependent on it every single second of the day. Very few understand that our daily happiness relies on external factors rather than content living. Do I have enough friends on Facebook? How many followers do I have on Instagram and Twitter? Why don't I have enough likes and comments on my posts? Why doesn't my life look like one of those photos from Pinterest? Why don't I look like the TikTok moms who have it all? Now, if Gen-X feels this way, I don't know what my Gen-Alpha children will go through by the time they are in middle school.

After reading multiple articles, listening to a podcast, doing deep mediation, and consistently thinking about the "happy zone bubble," I concluded that change has to start at home for my children's wellbeing. I have to be their role model by talking the talk and walk the walk. Creating my happy zone bubble, which includes everything that genuinely makes me feel joyful, was the way.

Even if the world disagrees with it, when we quiet our day by shutting down all the noise and listening to what our heart and mind have to say, we will understand who we are and what makes us happy. Knowing what we want and what makes us joyful is also based on our past experiences. But the best way to learn is to keep on asking yourself questions: How am I feeling? What makes me sad? What makes me happy? What do I need to do better in my life?

Simple questions will guide you to be a calmer person, and then it will be easy to create your happy zone bubble. Once you create a bubble that genuinely makes you feel more relaxed, joyful, satisfied, and content, live in this bubble for a while, and you will start attracting everything your heart desires.

Beauty Standards for Today's Woman

Anastasia Ciuntu

From time immemorial, womanhood has been considered a symbol of beauty. Across generations, the idea of a woman takes on new forms, with each era creating a certain standard. The angelic and innocent woman, the independent woman, and the mother-woman demonstrated the multitude of conditions in which the beauty of a woman is manifested.

Today, beauty is only a physical landmark. Society sometimes forgets that the mind and soul drive the body. Natural beauty is sometimes unappreciated by modern people, who choose perfect plastic. It was a refrain of a popular song. *Life in plastic it's fantastic / I'm a Barbie girl in a Barbie World.*

A women's desire to be desired has led, over time, to the obsession with cosmetic surgery. The fact that I do not know how to stop when I see how good I look in the mirror and how good I look after a specific procedure and the fact that other women choose to replace the natural with the unnatural that promises eternal beauty demonstrates how harmful it affects the human mentality. At present, a woman's body becomes an object that must be shaped by the pattern imposed by the society to which they belong.

Anorexia and bulimia can be common when trying to achieve this level of desired beauty. The idea that obesity or simple weight gain is assimilated with disgust and rejection is also imposed by the society in which we live but does not realize how much it hurts us. A person who falls outside standard beauty should never feel marginalized. We are not alone. We do not have to be. Humanity's struggle with beauty standards will be continuous and exasperating. Beauty can take many forms. You have to find the right one for you.

Women need to learn to accept and love themselves as they are. If many choose to use their minds and souls to see further, beyond the bodies and faces around them, beauty standards fall away. What is beauty? It is a myth for most. It is freedom for those who choose to see beyond what your body can offer.

Never Make a Woman Cry

Angelina Nădejde

Never make a woman cry
because her eyes are made to look at you with pleasure
when you come home.

Never make a woman cry
because she will forget to smile at you.
She will seal her mouth, and she will not be able to speak
words of love.

Never make a woman cry
because you will kill her dreams.
If her dreams die, it will be difficult for her to live
with hope.

Never make a woman cry
because you will hurt her heart
and her heart is made for love,
for her children and you.

Never make a woman cry
because she may too often look to death.

Her soul will die first, then her body.
You will want to hear her footsteps coming toward you,
you will long for her smile and her words of love.
But she will then be far too far away from you.

Women Who Changed My Life

Part II

Vesna Lucic

In 1994, I arrived in Toronto. I lived with my sister for a while. I had no idea what I was going to do. What type of job would I have? How would my life look? My English was in the early stages. American culture was completely foreign to me, and friends were seldom. I was like a tree removed from its place and ready to be replanted. Everything was at stake.

A friend of mine invited me to go to church. The next day, I sang in the church choir. Annually, choirs from all churches in North America would get together for the festival. Usually, festivals happen in the USA. After we had some refreshments, we took off to the Monastery of the Mother of God, which is about an hour's drive outside of Chicago. At the time of our arrival, the evening service was in full swing. Mother superior, Epraxia, greeted us and told us that we could retreat to our rooms if we were tired.

After prayer, we sat at a table with a priest and nun and conversed with them for 30 minutes. This was the first time in my life that I was in the Monastery and talking to a nun and priest-monk. When you stay in a monastery, the rule is to help them with work around Monastery, whatever is needed. Since I have experience in sewing, I assisted Mother Epraxia with making vestments in her shop. Everything was beautiful, well-made, and of elegant quality. There's nothing to add and nothing to subtract. Just perfect.

Mother Epraxia asked me, "What do you do for a living"? I said I make hats for ladies. Then she said nothing. The next time I worked with her, she asked me again, so what do you do for a living? I said, "I make hats for ladies." I wondered why she asked me again.

When Mother Epraxia suggested that I should make vestments, I recognized how wonderful that was. Before making ladies' hats, I did not work in a business before, and I would not know what Mother Epraxia was suggesting to me.

My daily living is surrounded by heavenly beauty making priestly vestments. God has mysterious ways of presenting what is best for us in our lives.

OMG

Ronald Rock

The winter of 1977-78 was one of the coldest and snowiest in my hometown's history. A total of 90 inches of snow fell over seventy-five days that winter. Temperatures were well below average, and strong northwesterly winds created the perfect environment for long stretches of lake effect snow and blizzard conditions.

In 1978, it was during such a blizzard when I had a brush with death. My friend and I had just registered for an evening class at our local high school and had squeezed into my 1972 Opel Manta, a small German-built sports coupe. The radio was blasting when my car quit moving across the railroad tracks.

Unbeknownst to me, the front wheels of the Opal had fallen into a large pothole immediately next to the rail. Through near whiteout conditions, I could see traffic traveling in both directions. Attempts to free the car by placing it in gear and rocking it back and forth were futile.

At some point, the railroad crossings had lowered, but I could not see them.

I knew these tracks were located on a bend, so I frequently glanced left and right, just in case. All I could see were the mercury-vapor lights reflecting brightly off the snow. After a few more glances, I noticed one of the lights moving more than usual. For some, seeing the light at the end of the tunnel is one of optimism. For others, it can be a train hurtling from the other direction. OH MY GOD!

With only seconds to react, adrenaline surged through me as I grabbed my friend by the collar. In one motion, I opened the car door and flung her past me. It was only then that I heard the train whistle wail over the radio. I rolled out immediately behind her as the train crashed into the car. The motion had thrown me clear.

As I was sprawled across the ground, I could feel the train wheels clicking across the rails only a few feet away.

As the train slowed to a stop, I had time to reflect and be thankful to God for sending me a guardian angel. This was my first real brush with death. I wasn't certain what God had planned for me, but I am eternally grateful for the opportunity to serve Him by serving others.

Stranger's Generosity

Luminita-Elena Stoenescu

I was heading home with my son after physical therapy. We had been on this side of town together for weekly physical therapy sessions because he needed unique treatments to strengthen his hip muscles. His gait was faulty, and he stepped over his own feet.

After the meeting, my son asked me to stop at the nearby pâtisserie and buy his favorite cake before we got home. I explained to him that I didn't have any spare cash, only the shopping card, but he didn't understand these differences. He was too small to understand.

We stopped and walked into the pâtisserie together. He went straight to the cake display and showed me the cake he wanted. There were a few people in the pâtisserie, two in front of a young man waiting for his turn and us. I showed the seller the cake and grabbed the card to make a payment, but unfortunately, the transaction could not be processed.

With sadness, I told my son that I couldn't buy the cake because that device didn't work, and I had no cash. Sadly, my son didn't say anything.

We turned to leave the shop, with both of us feeling embarrassed. Behind us followed the young man from the pâtisserie. He caught up with us and handed me a ten lei banknote. He said, "Please take these monies from me and buy the boy the cake. I insist!"

I shyly took the bill and thanked the young man for his lovely gesture. My son's face lit up. He happily reentered the pâtisserie and whispered to me, "What a good man! What a good man!"

Thus, I was taken out of the mess. My son learned from the young man that it is good to pay attention to the needs of the people around you and learned how wonderful it is to give to others when needed.

The generous young man cheerfully walked to the car, smiling at my son's joy and my gesture of gratitude.

I Am Driving!

Stamatoula P. Kretsedemas

I came as a 19-year-old young bride, and soon after, we welcomed our first child. Two more followed, and life was busy. I was not driving and dependent on my husband for everything from grocery shopping to taking our children to the doctor. It was not easy as he was working seven days a week.

I was frustrated and unhappy. I asked my husband to provide a translator for me to get my driver's license. I had heard that it was done in some circumstances, but I was unsure how true this was. He said to me that no one did it for him, who was also an immigrant, and he was not about to do it for me. Tough love, I guess. He brought me the book to read and told me, when I was ready, to go and take the test. My English was fair at best.

After some tears, I began to study. When I felt ready, I asked a friend to drive me to the DMV as I did not want to ask my husband in case I failed the test. When I got there, my husband coincidentally walked in to renew his license. I passed the tests and got my license. I was so happy and proud of my accomplishment, and so was my husband.

My life has been a continuous growing and learning experience. A good life lived in this special country.

Open Door of Opportunity

Luminita-Elena Stoenescu

I worked as a translator for a financial company, and I translated audit reports. The deadline was always "at the latest tomorrow."

I was young, single, and with grand ambitions. Working in front of the computer for countless hours and with my nose in dictionaries made me a bit isolated from the rest of my colleagues. My boss, Mrs. C, a woman with a strong personality, elegant and attractive, insisted that I come to work for her at her new company. We had been colleagues at another company. At first, everything went smoothly, and I tried not to disappoint her.

At home, to relax, I watched old movies and read. One day, I decided that I wanted to go to a school of theology. I told Mrs. C, and she agreed, and I couldn't be happier. I could have a job and study something that interested me. I studied intensely for two weeks and managed to be one of the first to enter college. I was a working student, but I didn't want to miss a course.

When I wasn't at school, I was at work. Mrs. C received a canon from her spiritual father to read six psalms for 40 days and asked me to read the psalms instead. I took her request seriously, so I began to read the psalms daily. Time passed, and we finished with the 40 days. Mrs. C. was not at the company, so I informed the CFO that I had an important exam to take during the morning and could not get to the company. The professor came from another university center twice a week, and I couldn't miss it. It was a written exam. But, at one point, one of my co-workers entered the classroom, telling me to come to the company urgently. I turned in my paper to the professor and left.

In the car, my colleague told me that Mrs. C was thundering and lightning. She said I put my work secondarily to my studies. When I arrived at the company, she didn't even want to look at me and told me to resign. I wanted to tell her that the 40 days had passed, but I didn't resist. I wrote the paper and signed it. She signed it, too. I took my things and left.

The following morning, I received a phone call from an international automotive company for an interview. I went to the interview, and I began my new job the next week. It was a better-paid job. One door slammed in my face and another opened wide.

Life is a mystery.

My Roots

Ioan Rosu

I spent most of my childhood in the country with my maternal grandparents because my parents divorced, and things didn't go well for us. That's how I grew up with my grandparents, Ioan and Maria. In their house, I gained an enormous love for what they meant for me. Unfortunately, when I was only six years old, my grandfather passed away, and I regret that he did not even live until I went to school for the first time.

I had evenings when my grandfather told me stories from when he was a child. He told me about the hardships he endured after his father's death and how he was raised by his paternal grandparents. During the day, I went with him through the garden, and he showed me the plants and the vines. He explained to me how to cut the vine and what care it needed. I accompanied him to the hives, even though I was terrified of bees that could sting me, but my grandfather calmed me down and provided everything I needed for protection. There in the hive, my grandfather showed me a queen who was moving very fast and who was surrounded and covered by the bees in her guard. Everything looked like a miniature village.

My grandmother used to cook for me what I wanted. The grandparents' garden was a real paradise, and it remains a paradise today. I liked it then as I like now to go to the garden and eat the fruits that ripen according to the season. I sometimes think about what it would be like if my grandfather was still living today and here with me.

But now, I try to enjoy the memories I have left of my grandfather. Today, as in the past, I listen to my grandmother's advice and learn from her.

I really want my grandmother to live at least until I enter college. I want to bring her the news and make her proud of how she raised me and guided me in life.

One other important person in my life is my aunt I live with and who takes care of me and provides for my daily needs. I love her like a mother because she does everything a mother has to do for her child. There are days when we contradict each other when our ideas do not align, and we need more arguments to clarify.

August

Asma Nooruddin

I married my husband when I was eighteen. Since we were both students at the time, we prioritized completing our studies over moving in together. His father sent him abroad to finish his Master's. Thus, my husband was the first member of his family to immigrate to the United States. After the long and exhausting plane ride, he felt incredibly homesick. All he wanted was lentils, rice, and a warm bed to sleep on. Luckily, the roommate who welcomed him to America served him just what he had been craving, lentils, rice, and a warm bed.

Back in Bangladesh, I was so worried about him. How was he faring all by himself in a foreign land? I asked when he called, and he cheerfully told me that he had cooked some chicken *biryani* for his friends. I realized then that he was doing just fine without me.

I joined my husband in Rapid City a year later. From the very first day I arrived, everyone greeted me with a smile. I was touched by this kind gesture and quickly fell in love with the small city.

Among my husband's peers, I was the only young bride. As the sole married couple, it was up to us to host our friends for Eid celebrations. It was the first time I had taken on such a big responsibility. We diligently kept up this tradition for thirty years until the coronavirus pandemic.

At some point, my husband became well-known for the *biryani* he would make for our guests. I enjoyed his cooking so much that I never bothered to make the dish myself. I even told him that if, God forbid, we were ever to divorce, I didn't want his money. I simply wanted him to send me some of his *biryani* from time to time. I felt life wasn't worth living without it.

A few years ago, my husband decided to serve spaghetti on Eid. The following Eid, a few friends of friends, showed up on our doorstep telling my children, "We heard the pasta here is delicious." We laughed. Never in our wildest dreams could we have imagined that the famous *biryani* would be upstaged by some spaghetti. I guess the comfort food of the younger generation is different from our own.

Their taste is undoubtedly American.

The Bean Dish

Eugen V. Rosu

In my early pastoral years, I met a man who was friendly and talkative. He was a storyteller. After many years spent in a steel mill as a troubleshooter, he could identify irregularities everywhere he looked. An electrical pole that was not perfectly straight. The wires were not stretched enough. The gutters were too close to the siding. The flowers were planted on the wrong side of the building. For his advanced age, he was very active. He kept up with everyone in the community, and everyone knew him. He would buy foods and drinks people liked and deliver them to their doorstep. He enjoyed giving gifts and seeing the smiles on people's faces.

One day, during the Great Lent, he approached me and asked about the right foods to eat during that time. I re-iterated the main aspect of fasting. Avoid all animal products. Eat only vegetables. The elderly, pregnant women and children are permitted to have animal products.

Then, he said that he could not stand beans without giving me a chance to ask why he continued. He told me about a time as a child when his mother cooked beans almost daily. Whenever he saw beans, he preferred to walk out and wander the streets.

Years had passed, and he enrolled in the army. The second world war took him as far as Indo-China. According to him, the soldiers were instructed to look for survival elements in the jungle if they were shot down. Soldiers were told to eat the same fruit that the monkeys ate. He saw the monkeys, but none of them were eating. After a while, he shot a monkey. When he ate the cooked meat of the monkey, he realized that he would rather have his mother's beans. The thought that those beans might have been tastier than the monkey made him tear up. Crying, he asked his mother for forgiveness for all the fuss he made when she prepared what the family could afford.

He said that beans were still not his favorite, but he learned not to refuse anyone's food because a well-cooked dish represents the love of that person. When someone offers food, that is not just a dish of meat and vegetables; it is the labor of love of someone who stood for some time to prepare it.

Immediately, he excused himself because he needed to take some root beer to a friend.

Flowers

Angelina Nădejde

People are like flowers.
The world is full of flowers.
Like flowers, we live and die.

I know people like perennial flowers,
these are my friends.
Winters pass,
springs come, and they are by my side.

All they need is for me to keep them close,
as the flowers need to be watered
from time to time.

Others are like flowering weeds.
They live only for themselves,
drawing strength from the sap of the earth,
and they die without regret
of those around.

But some
are

flowering peonies.
You can feel them burning
for others.

They give love,
peace,
and serenity.
These are the real flowers.

Being Happy

Andrei Cristian Mateescu (12 years old)

Happiness is a beautiful feeling you must take advantage of because you can have it so easily and lose it just as quickly.

Talent? It's a gift from birth, one you should not take advantage of. The greatest sin in life is wasted talent.

The soul represents the armor of man, which can hold in it many sufferings and joys. Defend it.

Money? No one takes you seriously if you do not have it. It is something important in society.

Games are moments of joy. Games are the magic of childhood. And childhood is something unique and wonderful. It is said that it lasts 18 years, but some people keep their souls as a child even when they grow old.

A house is a special place. There, you feel good and make memories of all kinds.

Sadness is the sunset of happiness. It is a part of life. You cannot do without it.

Journey to My Ancestral Roots

David M. Oancea

During my childhood, my family took short summer vacations, usually no more than a week at a time. My dad, an educator, had summers off, but he always worked two or three jobs, so he arranged vacation time with some difficulty.

We often visited Liviu and his family in Michigan. My dad and Liviu escaped from Romania when communism first started to take root in their homeland. This event in my dad's youth and the fascinating journey that brought him to North America became an integral part of his identity and, in turn, part of mine.

My dad was a very social person. He loved to have people over to our house and visit friends on Sunday afternoons with the whole family. During these visits, the conversation inevitably gravitated to my dad's escape as a teenager. I heard the story numerous times. He was a first-rate storyteller, able to remember minute details, making the listener feel as if they were present with him.

Only after 1989, when communism fell, did my dad consider returning to his homeland with my mom. His first visit back reunited him with family members he had not seen for over 40 years. It was a joyous reunion.

In 1997, I invited him to travel with my wife and daughter on my first trip to Romania. He gladly agreed to accompany us. We visited my relatives and the village near where my dad's home used to be. I felt at home. I felt like I belonged in that place. My dad retold the story of his and Liviu's escape, and I recorded it on film. For the first time, the story I had heard so many times came to life in front of me.

This journey to my ancestral roots impacted me on every level. Although only a 5-week vacation, one of the few I've taken in my adulthood, it became for me the journey of a lifetime. This journey forged a deep and lasting connection with my dad and his origins, my ancestral roots.

Overcoming Adversity

Brenda Whillock

When I was growing up, it was not easy; at the time, it felt like everyone else had the perfect life, family, and situation. I know now as an adult that is not true; everyone has struggles. How we choose to deal with them can change our life for better or worse. I moved a lot, my parents divorced when I was very young, and my mom remarried a few times.

With each marriage came instability and adversity for my sister and me. We had each other, and at times that felt like enough, but then life and people showed us just how different we were. We did not have much money and were teased about the clothes we wore and the broken-down car we drove. There were many defining moments throughout my childhood that I can say molded me into the adult I am today, but one, in particular, feels like yesterday, so vivid in my memory that it feels like I am there again.

There was a girl that would go out of her way to bully and pick on me. I had enough and decided to stand up for myself. She met me after school with many of her friends, and I guess to beat me up, or so she thought. I was terrified but knew it would not end if I did not stand up to her. In the middle of the taunting and teasing, all of a sudden, she and her friends retreated and left. Imagine my relief. As I turned around, I saw why -- there was my sister and her friends who had come to rescue me. To this day, I don't know how my sister knew about it; she was in high school down the road from my middle school; regardless, I was so glad to see her there. That is just one of many stories of overcoming adversity. I have become a much stronger person, and I will always choose to be the victor and not the victim. As I go through life and meet more people, I see that everyone has struggles to overcome. We need to be there for each other like my sister was there for me.

A Thankful Decision

Lori Foley-Jacquez

It was late June 2020 when my elderly aunt informed me she might have contracted the Covid-19 virus. The first week she stayed home isolated, dealt with the symptoms, and believed she would be fine in a few days. After the first week, the symptoms subsided, yet she still had some cough issues. By the end of that week, my aunt seemed to be getting worse. The cough had moved deep into her lungs, and she was getting worse by the day. For the next couple of days, I brought her meals and checked on her. I could tell she was becoming more and more lethargic. Her fever continued to spike as well. When her fever reached 103, and her overall acuity was declining, I called her doctor and explained to him that her cough began sounding bad, almost like pneumonia.

The doctor's immediate response surprised me. He said to take her to the hospital emergency room and admit her because there was no treatment, he could give her due to the virus. I shared what the doctor had said with my aunt, and she also agreed there was nothing that could be done, but she refused to be admitted to the hospital. I also shared with her that she may need to get some antibiotics to help out with the increasingly bad cough. I called her doctor once again, explaining she declined the hospital; his response was the same. I pleaded with him to prescribe her an antibiotic or something that may help her declining state. He refused, telling me over and over that nothing would help, that it was a virus. I immediately began calling urgent care facilities, other doctors, and PAs, asking if they could see her and hopefully prescribe something to help out. I was finally able to reach a nurse who found a "Covid Patient Only Clinic."

My aunt's appointment was scheduled for the following day, but honestly, I didn't know if she would make it through the night. She was seen by a Physician's Assistant who confirmed she had a nasty case of pneumonia; she prescribed her an antibiotic, an inhaler, and cough medicine. Within a few hours of taking the medication, she could take a deep breath and be on the mend. I am grateful for the Physician's Assistant who did try and who made a difference for my aunt. I am a true believer in never giving up when you know something is not quite right!

The Day I Got My Dog

Ana Maria Rosu (9 years old)

My mom, my dad, and I got in the car going somewhere to meet someone. After driving for almost half an hour, we stopped at a gas station. I saw a car parking next to ours. I didn't know who the car belonged to, but my parents did. I didn't understand why we were going to the other vehicle, but soon I found out.

It was a surprise. I had been waiting for about one year. I was getting my dog! I was so excited to hold Dixon in my arms for the first time. He was tiny and fluffy. After that, we got back in our car we drove home. On the way home, Dixon slept on my lap. He is the most adorable dog. Now we play every day. When we go out for a walk, he likes to run and mark every tree and bush. I spend a lot of time with my puppy. Sometimes I read to him, and he listens until he wants to play, and then he barks. I thanked my parents for the big surprise.

The Opportunity For Change

Bassam Matar

Civil war and corruption still plague my home, a tiny village in the Middle East. For twenty-five years, my father worked on another continent to provide for my mother and her four children. Neither parent made it past third grade. My mother never learned to read, write, or drive. This was all common in my village. We became the more fortunate ones because of their plan.

My parents wanted more for their children. Education was the answer. My dad's choice to leave the family bought my education halfway around the world—in the U.S.A. There were two choices, medical doctor, or engineer.

At 18 years old, I landed at the airport alone, not knowing any English. I'll never forget the anxiety of trying to find my way to the right terminal and gate. I just waved my paperwork in front of anyone that looked official.

My first destination was quite a shock. I didn't expect the kind of reception I got, as it seemed many didn't like my kind. More than a few times, I packed my bags and planned how to get back home, where there was the comfort of family and my mother's food.

I didn't have an easy way to communicate with her. Telephone service didn't exist in my village. Just to speak with me for a few expensive minutes, my mother would have to taxi to a small city one hour away. Otherwise, I would send word through cassette tape with anyone going that way.

I studied English for six months. For a while, I survived on the same food, ordered over and over, because I could not speak English. I laugh when I think back on it.

For one year at a time, I received a humble-sized stipend from my father to take care of my academic and personal needs—tuition, books, rent, car, gas, food, clothes, etc. He trusted me. I wasn't going to let my family down.

From community college to university, earning my master's degree in Electrical Engineering meant that eventually, I would be able to support my family, attempting to pay back the sacrifices my parents made.

Now, I'm guiding my children to be good citizens and get their education too. I was the first generation.

Friendship

Eugen V. Rosu

He was a cute four-year-old boy. Active, creative, and very funny. He asked me to go to the game room and play with him on the first visit. To make sure I would go with him, he grabbed my hand. There, he had a few favorite toys and books. He handed me a book about a train. I read the book to him and changed my voice for each character. He laughed with his whole body. Reading and playing with him relaxed me and made me feel good.

After that day, I made a habit of stopping every day to visit him in the early afternoon. He waited for me. He could not tell the time, but he knew it was after his lunch. We built blocks. We colored papers. He was very particular about what color things should be.

On a Friday afternoon, we played and read stories. He told me how much he likes how I change my voice for different characters. He looked into my eyes and said that he would read just like me one day. When he wanted to make sure that I listened to him, he grabbed my face still and looked me straight on. I don't know if he saw me as his friend, but, for me, he was a dose of joy and happiness. Time had different dimensions when I was with him.

I said "goodbye" to him and went to see another patient. As I was getting ready to leave for the day, one nurse asked me where my friend was. I answered her that I had left him in the room. We went to look back in the room, and he was not there. The entrance to the unit was closed. No one could get in, and no one could get out. We checked every room in the department. He was nowhere to be found.

I went back into the room, and I said out loud, "If I read one more story to you, will you come out of your hiding spot?"

Slowly, he came out from a place where none of us had looked. He came to me in tears and asked me not to leave him because I was his best friend. He tightly locked his arms around my neck. We remained friends for the time he was in the hospital.

I am sure that today he is someone else's friend. He is a good friend.

The Other Face of Justice

Silvia Grigore

"**M**embers of the jury, stand up and present the verdict."

"Following the administration of the law, the panel deliberated in the name of the law and decided to condemn the two defendants to eighteen years in prison each for deprivation of liberty and culpable homicide."

I feel that the sky has fallen on my head. Eighteen years in prison!

The lawyers left. There is a murmur in the room, and someone shouts at me, "Madam Journalist, do you think that's fair? What will you write about this case?"

I cannot answer the man, and only now do I realize that I am facing the most complicated case of my entire career. The deed happened, the evidence was analyzed correctly, the charges were correct, and the punishment was as provided by law. And yet, from a moral point of view, it is outrageous.

Gogu, a drunkard with no head and no desire to work terrorized the whole community more than twenty years ago in a small village. He entered people's households at night and stole food, clothes, and drinks. He always had a paralyzing spray and a knife with him, so people would let him steal rather than risk their lives. Complaints to the police always remained unresolved.

Costin was a hardworking man with a hardworking wife and two beautiful children. One morning he found that his tool shed had been broken into, and his things were missing. Later, he discovered they were missing two turkeys. One night, he decided to stand guard and catch the thief. When the drunkard came to him in the yard, Costin wrapped his legs with a rope in a single movement; then, together with his wife, Mariana, they took the thief's knife and spray and tied him to his hands and feet, next to a tree. They went into the house, aware that the police would come in a few hours.

Only destiny took an unexpected turn. When the police arrived, Gogu was found dead! At the autopsy, it was determined that he had developed a severe lung disease due to the thief's tobacco use and a drinking problem. The time that he had spent on the cold ground in a fixed position exacerbated his lungs and caused his death.

It has been over twenty years since Gogu's death. I have thought about this controversial case many times. Two parents were in prison. Their two children were left at an orphanage. It was unjust.

A Temporary Guest

Luminita-Elena Stoenescu

One summer, when I was 12 and still living with my parents and younger sister, a bird flew in through the open kitchen window. Although the kitchen window was often left open, the bird, who we named Sulfi, did not want to leave from that day on. We all came to love her. She slept in my room above the bookshelves, and in the morning, she would fly and hop around and sing for us. She wasn't afraid of me, and we became inseparable. She would sit on my shoulder or in my palm. She drank water from the kitchen faucet, and everything was more beautiful with her around.

But, one day, when I got home from school, my mother told me that Sulfi had flown out the kitchen window and had apparently decided to leave us.

For weeks, I felt great pain. When I returned from school, I would walk around the block and yell for her. I wanted her to hear my voice and fly to my shoulder, but this did not happen. I did not understand why she stayed with us for so long or why, one day, she suddenly wanted to leave.

Many years later, when I was a teenager in college, I found out what happened to Sulfi. I was with my relatives at the table, and after we shared funny stories, I brought up Sulfi. My mother revealed to me that Sulfi was dead because she ate dishwashing detergent that had been left open on the kitchen sink. My parents did not want to tell me because they did not want me to suffer. Instead, they decided to explain to me that she had flown out the window.

For years, I saw Sulfi with the eyes of the living. She wasn't here, but at least she was happy, flying from branch to branch. This revelation from my mother made everything take a sudden turn. My mother had answered a question I had had since childhood. The thought that Sulfi had not abandoned me brought me a certain comfort, but I was very sorry for my negligence of not putting away the dishwashing detergent. I can't turn back time, and I can't change the deeds I did.

Nettles

Luminita-Elena Stoenescu

Since I was a child, I have liked to move my hand among the nettles. I only felt well after the sting of the nettles began to drop slightly. Someone saw me with my hand in the nettles and exclaimed, "Look, there is someone who caresses the nettles!" I found that remark funny, and every time I touch the customs, I remember those words.

I was on the alley leading to the Old Church in England, near the North Sea. It was nice outside. The nuns and I strolled down the alley guarded on either side by green nettle bushes. I remembered the nettle soup with rice my grandmother would make and told the nuns of that childhood memory.

The mother cook of the monastery told us that it sounded nice and that today, we would eat nettles. Later that day, she brought us three big bags and three pairs of rubber gloves and asked us to fill the nets with nettles. I refused to take the gloves because I wasn't afraid of nettles.

I picked them up with my bare hands, but after I had filled only half of the net, the pain became more and more unbearable, so I grabbed the gloves. My right hand numbed like a stone. I could feel millions of needle pricks in my hand. I took off my gloves in vain. The pain persisted. I couldn't even eat with my right hand. Seeing me in pain, someone brought me a bowl of vinegar to soak my hand. It took many hours for the pain to pass.

At the dinner table, Father Abbot poured the nettled from the plate into the bowl. Seeing him, I imagined that my grandmother's recipe was not to his liking and that my desire to share something dear to me was considered something worthless.

After returning home to my country, my husband drove a priest and spoke with him in his car. My husband later told me that the priest talked excitedly about nettles in the car and said, "tell your wife to pick nettles and make nettle food." This priest recommended nettles as a valuable gift from God.

We often see people making and can only imagine what they think and intend. Things are driven by an imagination devoid of understanding of reality.

Alone In An Ocean of People

Mariana Alexandradescu

An honest day begins and ends with real problems: with children, with back pain, with the telephone company, with the car, with the neighbors, with the traffic, with love.

The daily bombardment consumes my energy, attenuates my normal reactions and emotions, blurs my perception, and gives rise to surprising answers, themselves sources of other questions.

Empty and dry, I lock my soul so that it is not disturbed by an honest look or smile, by a dumb pain or wretched helplessness because I discovered a fascinating world, in a sweet self-isolation, a click away.

I open it impatiently when my real world stays behind my actual closed door. Messages, comments, flowers, and hearts are offered in virtual abundance by so many "friends" in the space that covers, geographically, the entire planet's surface, waiting for an equally consistent response, demanding my time, energy, and emotions.

And here I am in the service of all evenings and nights, subject to the sweet virtual drug, my magical world, with countless friends.

I don't care who the neighbor is who leaves me a rose at the door every day, or the colleague who sends me tickets, the stranger I meet daily and looks at me insistently, or the lady who wants to tell me about her missing daughter from home or the child with the so sad face I have been meeting for a few nights on my way home.

It is infinitely more exciting to discover who is the mysterious M, from the end of the world, who sends me virtual roses, the erudite Z, who captivates me with philosophical discussions, and the conqueror X, which makes me dizzy with tempting promises or the charming Y who melts me with compliments!

How close was happiness! Which I have to give up in exchange for a few hours of sleep and a new day in an objective and dull world, again oversaturated with problems. I feel more and more distant and alienated, part of the paradox of society, loneliness in an ocean of people.

I am looking forward to the virtual excitement of the opening of my wonderful world. It is one click away!

Summer Day

Em Sava

It is a summer day. I'm in the garden working. It's as if I've just discovered the convenience of the garden. We haven't been out so long since we bought our house. And that happened seven years ago.

I like the idea of greenery without being a gardening fan. Since I moved my office into the garden, writing has flowed like hot honey. It's like someone turned on the tap. I love the static emerald of nature, and the green joy interrupted from time to time by a scary squirrel or a red and musical cardinal. Sometimes you hear neighborhood noises. The Babylon of the city sits boldly on every street. There are areas with a solid ethnic personality, but it is pretty colorful here.

A syrtaki is heard. Someone is feeling well. I don't think it's a party. It's Monday night. But it's a good thing. Maybe there is a message hidden in the song. I do not know. It's a gust of wind that brings the music close, and a butterfly crosses a few meters from me. I was sure that my screens were upset in the sun, and I would not see them working, but the thick vine above is a generous ceiling that does not let the sun's rays interrupt or disturb me. I think that the slight antipathy towards the garden comes from the beginning when, wanting to water the flowers in the morning, I woke up with a skunk a few meters from me.

We understood that he lived here in front of us, strategically located between our shed and the neighbor's, sitting back-to-back with the fence that delimits our properties between them. The skunk made its nest somewhere between them, almost impossible to reach. Smart boy. That morning I was half-asleep when I just saw him with his tail up in the attack. I disappeared like teleported, screaming for my brave neighbor. He came and looked for him, but he was gone—not as fast as I was, though.

Ahh, let's say I've been scared to death for a long time. However, it was a team that transported him to a better area. But who knows? What if he misses his little house under the fence?

The Woman and Her Flowers

Luminita-Elena Stoenescu

In the center of a city, an older woman sat outside a building with a wicker basket full of wildflower bouquets. She was selling them to earn money. The older woman smiled at passersby, who looked at the beautiful bouquets in the basket at her feet. Now and then, young girls would stop to buy a colorful bouquet. The older woman did not force people to stop at her basket. She just waited patiently by her flowers.

As I watched her from a nearby bench under the shade of an oak, I was curious to know the story of this wildflower woman's life.

After a while, I got up and headed to the older woman. I engaged with her. The older woman did not feel embarrassed by my questions. She answered me kindly, providing details of her life. The older woman told me that she was homeless. She slept under the starry sky and picked wildflowers to have a few pennies to eat. She had sold her apartment to give her son money to buy a house with his wife. Her son and his wife seemed excellent and beautiful. They promised to take care of her and built a room outside the big house for her in the yard.

For several years, things went well until the young couple divorced. The woman's daughter-in-law didn't want to know about her anymore. They sold the house, and the woman stayed in the yard. The son moved in with another woman, and the older woman did not want to enter their lives.

I was moved by the sad story of the older woman's life and felt sorry for her careless son. Wanting to help her, I gave her a considerable sum of money, but the older woman did not want to take the money. She just wanted to sell the wildflowers. Seeing that I insisted, she finally accepted the money on the condition that I take all the flowers with me.

A few months later, I found out that the older woman had arrived at an older people's home in a village near the city, living with people with broken hearts like her.

Let's Go!

Elena Lupu

"Let's go!"

"Let's go? Where?"

"To the mountains!"

Said and done. The young couple set off, each with a backpack on their back and their clothes, with restlessness on his face and a slight confusion on her face; the young people started their journey. The goal was to climb one of the most famous mountain peaks in their region. This task was not so easy to accomplish.

In the morning, with fresh forces and coolness in the air, it left them with the impression of an adventure easier to conquer than they would have expected. But, like life, even a mountain road comes with its sudden surprises. Here a calm rain with tiny drops reaches their skin. There was a sun burning in the clouds as if it would be his last chance to leave them with tanning marks on their face. Beyond, a cliff so steep that it leaves them with a knot in their throats until long after they see themselves at the top. But when you reach the top, what a moment of joy!

The truth is, they didn't get to talk that much. The physical exertion had reduced them to indistinct grunts, sighs, glances, and short smiles from time to time. It's just that now they didn't seem to need that many words. They shared the same joy and were aware of it. They were conscious of their success but also aware that they got there together. Now all they had to do was live that moment. To see the beauty of the road that almost left them breathless. To see how the cliffs they didn't think they would cross can now be seen as foaming waves ready to break into the beach of old fir trees on the coast. To see how the sun now caresses them and the wind soothes the scratches on their arms and legs.

Now she was happy. And he needed a moment of confusion to understand why. Now they were happy together. They were glad to be where they were at that time. And to his surprise, this time she said:

"Let's go!"

"Let's go? Where?"

"Down, the road doesn't stop here. We have another trip."

Constantin

Eugen V. Rosu

It was a crisp October morning. Constantin prepared his eight-and-a-half-year-old brother and seven-year-old sister for school. They ate breakfast of one egg and a slice of bread each. Constantin was almost eleven years old.

His parents were gone working in another European country to raise enough money to build a farm. Before his siblings took off to school, he gave them strict instructions. He told his brother, Dimitrie, to look after their dog and feed it twice a day. He told his sister, Elena, to be careful and not fall in her small boots. His sister remarked that she didn't have to remember all of these instructions because Constantin was there for her.

They took off. The narrow path was muddy, but there were footmarks in the mud from other people walking on it, and so the two kids tried to jump on those dried spots.

Constantin took a deep breath and went into the house accompanied by his dog. He picked up the phone and called his mother for the second time that day. He received a text two days before in which his mother told him that they would talk soon. He wasn't able to speak with her for the past four days and was worried.

He left a message for his mother, "Mama, I have been calling you for four days, and I cannot talk with you. I don't know what is happening to you and tata. When the two of you left a year ago and had grandma supervise us, she got sick, and I had to take care of her, too. You told me that now I am the man of the house. Mama, I am tired. I don't want to be the man of the house anymore. I want to go back to school and play with my friends. I want to play soccer. I don't want you to bring me any toys or games. I want you back. I love you."

He turned off the phone and set it on the kitchen table. He went into the barn, picked up the rope, and went to the walnut tree. At the same time, his mother called back, but there was no answer. She and her husband entered the courtyard calling for their son. They went into the garden, where the dog barked desperately. As they got closer, the mother screamed, "Constantineeee!"

A Good Man

Angelina Nădejde

I believe that good people are born good,
they do not become.
They are molded out of the love
of two twin souls
and out of God's love.

A man's kindness is seen in words,
gestures,
silences.
You feel it in the way
he greets you, telling you
good morning
like the ringing of a bell
or good evening like
comfort to your soul.

He always smiles, and his smile
is like the opening of a budding flower.
He hugs us and does it
as if God embraces
the earth with his arms.

A good man makes your day bright.
He is comforting when you meet him,
like a summer rain
over the scorched earth.

He is sent to earth
to lift us when we are
brought down to our knees
by worry, disease, and despair.
He does all of these
in God's stead.

A Miracle of Healing

Cornel Todeasa

Most miracles do not follow human reasoning and escape our understanding. I witnessed one that left me wondering, and it is one I will never forget.

Silvia was very ill and in the Intensive Care Unit. Her kidneys had stopped working, and the doctors had given her 24 hours to live. The family was devastated, for she was still young. It was hard for them to see her in such great pain. Silvia was in agony but aware of all that was happening.

I prayed with her, and she received Holy Communion. Almost immediately, she returned to life. Her kidneys began working again, and the color returned to her face. We all saw this miracle, Sylvia included. She was full of joy for receiving such grace from God and told everyone who came to visit about how the Lord had made her well.

However, the miracle that took place in the ICU was only temporary, and her return to life was not long-lasting. Within two months, she passed. Questions flooded my mind. Why would God perform a miracle that was so short-lived? After searching my heart, I realized that this miracle was to help Silvia with her death and salvation. She was not a strong believer by any means. After the Lord touched her in this unique way, she was completely transformed.

She found joy in the Lord. She trusted the Lord. She felt His power and was not afraid of anything anymore, not even death.

The miracle of Silvia's healing should be a divine lesson for all of us. It was for me. When I finally understood God's reason for it, I praised and glorified Him with all my heart, all my mind, and with all my soul. Let us pray with Saint Paul for "the work of faith with power, that the name of our

Lord Jesus Christ may be glorified in you, and you in Him, according to the grace of our God and the Lord Jesus Christ" (2 Thessalonians 1:10-12). The grace of God is concerned first and foremost with the salvation of our souls. Through the miracle wrought by prayer and the Holy Eucharist, Silvia connected anew with her Creator, and He shepherded her into His bosom.

Making Time

Cornel Todeasa

"...I Don't Have the Time."

I remember a parishioner who said to me, "I'm sorry I can't come to church often, but I'm so busy. I don't have the time."

So I asked her, "Why don't you have the time?"

She replied, "I have to do this, go here, buy something, take this, bring that, etc."

I replied, "It seems you have time for everything except God."

We are very good at finding excuses, and "not having enough time" is the most-used excuse. The fact that my friend cannot find time for God — Who gives her all the time she has — is beyond comprehension. How quickly we forget that time is not ours but God's.

Jesus himself illustrated these same types of excuses in the parable of the banquet (Luke 14:16-24). When the banquet was ready and the invited guests were asked to come, many sent their regrets. With a bit of humor, the parable lists three excuses, all related to "not having enough time." I don't have time because "I have bought a field, and I must go out and see it." I don't have time because "I have bought five yokes of oxen, and I must go to examine them." I don't have time, for "I have married a wife, and therefore, I cannot come."

Who is the giver of all these good things? God is the Giver. He gave the invited guests the field, the oxen, and the wife. He also gave them the time to enjoy their gifts. We can see by their excuses that the invited guests put their material gifts as well as the gift of time above the Giver.

God will not suffer our excuses. He knows the truth, just as He knows us and our inner motives. The invited guests were excluded from the banquet and excluded from the Kingdom: "For I tell you, none of those men who were invited shall taste of my banquet."

For the things that we want or like, we find the time. We should remember, then, that there is nothing more important for us than God. We must give Him time, for all that we give Him — whether it is our time, talents, or love — is only giving back what is His.

Modern Slaves

Em Sava

Today, the power was turned off for two hours. I had just returned from my daily shift. My routine is to start my day with a walk in the neighborhood while talking to my mother.

Half asleep, I ignored the big trucks in front of the house. I saw that they were working, but I noticed that they were packed with a lack of electricity only thirty minutes later. Returning from the walk, I wanted to make my coffee, but I could neither grind the coffee nor use the filter. The stove, also electric, was not helpful to me. I remembered that I had a box of ness from time immemorial, which I kept for other purposes. I weighed the two possibilities: make a ness or walk in the heat of early August to get coffee. The ness won.

I took some water, but the filter in the fridge was, of course, mute. It did not work either. I turned on tap water and added sugar and black powder until I made a somewhat drinkable drink. But the most painful was the internet. While working from home, I need to be connected at least during business hours. I decided to write some articles, but of course, the laptop was almost dead. All the appliances in the house were silent and frozen in the position where the current had found them—as if in a stop-game of civilization. The refrigerator had a dark mouth, and I quickly closed the door to keep the temperature low. The clothes dryer was switched off, and the dishwasher was no longer squeaking.

The house was quiet at the beginning of time, and I felt completely helpless as if someone had unscrewed both my hands and I should have been able to do without them.

I was sorely missing my routine: the Netflix that had always accompanied me at breakfast, the quick Facebook tour, checking emails, emergencies that needed to be resolved, and a bunch of small things that I usually do not care about.

In the quiet of the house, I felt panicked. I did not know what to do with myself, as if I had been unplugged, just like the machines around me. I realized how dependent we are on machines that make our lives easier, mainly because we are just slaves—slaves to the comfort and sophistication of the lives we live in.

October

Asma Nooruddin

During our marriage, my husband and I lived in a total of four states. From South Dakota, we moved to Texas, where we welcomed our eldest son. Then, we moved to California, where we welcomed our only daughter and our youngest son. When they were old enough to start going to school, we moved once more to Arizona.

We wanted a natural birth for all three of our children. My parents were unable to attend my first delivery. Therefore, the support I received from my friends meant the world to me. The nurses, in particular, were like angels sent from above. I will never forget their gentleness and professionalism as they carried me through this life-changing transition into parenthood.

When my husband saw our first child, he was amazed at how beautiful a newborn can be. I remember how I was tending to our baby after returning from the hospital when my husband waltzed into the bedroom and carried our son out to introduce the baby to his friends. In his excitement, my husband didn't realize I still hadn't finished swaddling our child. If you have ever been around newborns, you'll know they look silly when they are not bundled up properly. Nevertheless, our friends doted over him.

Before my husband even mentioned the idea of going to Arizona, I had a dream. In it, I was living in a neighborhood where the houses all had terracotta-colored roofs. For some reason, this impression felt significant. When we finally arrived in Arizona, I was astonished to see the buildings exactly like what I had envisioned in my dream.

I later told my husband that I wanted to settle down here. I have never lived for a longer time in any one region than I have in this wonderful state. Naturally, it has become dear to me. While my nuclear family was scattered around the world, I was lucky to have my aunt and uncle nearby. They became close confidants for my husband and me and sources of inspiration for my children. I genuinely believe the guidance I received from my elders strengthened my family.

They say home is not only where your grandparents were born but also where your children are raised. By the grace of God, Arizona has become my home.

Mother's Tattoos

Silvia Grigore

Mirela grew up in a family without possibilities. Her parents loved her, but they could not afford to send her to school. So, she resigned herself to the fact. She got a job in a supermarket. She later got married and soon gave birth to a girl named Catalina.

Fate did not smile at Mirela even in marriage. Abandoned by her husband, she raised the little girl alone. She suffered and cried, thinking that, like her parents, she would not have the money to send her daughter to school.

Catalina proved to be incredibly talented at drawing. She went to art high school, and in the last year, she participated in a contest and won. There, she was noticed by the owner of a large beauty salon. Seeing Catalina's creative potential, she discovered that Catalina would not go to college due to a lack of money. After high school, the woman offered to pay for a professional tattoo course for Catalina, provided she worked at her salon after.

Catalina accepted, finished high school among the top in her class, and went to professional tattoo classes. She learned a great deal but felt that she did not get enough practice.

She did not plan to go work at the salon without becoming better at her sketching tattoos. Tattoos were very fashionable, but something held her back. Seeing Catalina upset, her mother offered herself as a model. She let her daughter tattoo her arms, thighs, and back. Catalina retouched Mirela's eyebrows, eyelids, and lips. Everyone wondered what was happening to her and why she resorted to something like that, especially where Mirela got the money for tattoos.

The day came when Catalina felt confident in her tattoo artistry, and she went to the salon to work. Catalina became famous in the city for her tattoos in a brief time. She raised the prestige of the salon and, from time to time, even appeared on TV for her talents.

Catalina found success and was making money. She bought a modern house and moved in with her mother.

Now, Mirela is happy. It was just yesterday that people pointed the finger at her, saying that it is not appropriate to allow such vanity at her age. Today, she is a respected woman because everyone knows and understands the sacrifice she had made for Catalina. Tattoos are painful, but for your daughter, you would make the sacrifice for her.

Fathers Lose Babies Too

Ronald Rock

My wife and I were both medical professionals expecting our second child, a boy. Everything was going well until my wife's water unexpectedly broke at 24 weeks. She was admitted into the hospital, where she remained bedbound for the next four weeks. Day in and day out, we were hoping and praying for a miracle.

On Christmas Day, she no longer felt any movement. An ultrasound confirmed what we had feared most. The frustration and feelings of helplessness were overwhelming as my wife was induced to deliver a stillborn child.

Several months later, she became pregnant again with another boy. This pregnancy progressed without any immediate concerns. We were both cautiously optimistic. A close friend performed a routine ultrasound. During the procedure, my wife sensed a problem when friendly conversation abruptly stopped. Her friend's face and eyes transformed from friend to concerned professional. It revealed a large build-up of fluid in the baby's brain, a missing kidney, and a remaining kidney covered in cysts. These conditions were incurable and would ultimately be fatal to the child. They also put my wife's health in danger.

We had lengthy discussions with numerous medical specialists. Going to term was out of the question. The baby would never survive. The long-term prognosis was bleak. Risks to my wife's health were high. There was a lot of information to process. After talking to our priest, we made the incredibly difficult decision to abort.

There was some comfort for me being by my wife's side during these challenging times. I found some relief in supporting her the best way I could. There was little I could do but focusing on her distracted me from my grief. Unfortunately, for the second time now, I couldn't imagine what was going through my wife's mind, not to mention the emotional and psychological toll it was taking on her.

My faith in God was severely tested. We had done everything right. Were we being punished for taking a life? Would we ever have any more children? Our faith and marriage were strong, and, despite our tremendous heartache, we continued to pray for strength, forgiveness, and guidance.

Our prayers were answered with the blessing of two children, two girls, who made our lives unimaginably beautiful.

The Forgotten Book

Luminita-Elena Stoenescu

In high school, I wanted to study a foreign language in a city with possibilities. I trained with good teachers in high school to do so. My French teacher spoke in an elegant way that fascinated me. I wanted to be like her. She was a distinguished and highly cultured person.

After an interesting discussion one morning, she told me that I look like a character from a book by a great writer, Olguța. She lent me four volumes written by Olguta and told me to read them. I got home and began reading right away. The books were just as interesting and captivating as the teacher had described them. Gradually, I read them and then placed them nicely in my library once I was done.

After a while had passed, the teacher asked me if I still had the books. I said they were not with me. I did so with shame. The teacher was gentle with me, did not insist on the volumes, and never mentioned the four volumes again.

Years passed. I arrived as I had wanted at the college in the city with possibilities, but I often regretted my choice during high school. Although I later changed my mind and tried to return the books, I could not because the French teacher had left the country and moved to France. No one knew her address. To amend what I had done in the past, I shared the books with different people.

After 30 years, I thought about the books and my old French teacher. To my delight, I found her. She was retired and living in France. She now had Parkinson's disease. I contacted her. She remembered me fondly, and I confessed my thoughtless gesture all those years ago and apologized.

It took me 30 years to track down the borrowed books. The teacher told me, "Books are for reading and for circulating among people." A comforting word that does not erase the gesture I made in high school.

The things we once did remain imprinted as a seal in the memory of our hearts.

The Magical Box

Dana Fodor Mateescu

I close my eyes, and I see her. Small, strange, shiny, made of a ceramic material, rounded at the corners. A box.

Grandma won't let me play with her, so I won't ruin her. She doesn't even let me touch her. God, how the doll sitting in the box attracted me! I dreamed of it day and night.

One day, my father was looking for something in the box. I reached out to touch her. Father let me do whatever I wanted. He took her out of the junk box. That box was the world beyond. A world of the dead. It frightened me but also attracted me terribly.

The doll did not have a leg. Only the head and palms were made of porcelain. The dress, which had been white when it was made, had lace ruffles. She was a princess.

I expected her to say something. Her eyes, azure, with long, curled eyelashes, looked at me as if she were alive. Her cherry mouth laughed a little, revealing two pearls for teeth. Her curls were blond.

"Is she a child?"

"Probably."

I was in the middle of moving her when I heard a noise coming from behind her. Dad shook her and took a strange box from behind the doll.

"What is that?" I asked.

"Hmmm, it looks like a music box," my father said.

He took what he was looking for from the box and put the doll back in place. He put the music box in his pocket and put his index finger to his lips. That meant Grandma didn't have to know.

I jumped up in joy!

In the box was a tiny ebonite disc with channels and dashes. I am certain that my father repaired it for me. It brought the 1930s to the 1970s.

It worked when I shook it. There was a child's roar of laughter from the disk as we played it. My father read from the box that it was recorded in the '20s and '30s. He was enjoying the discovery of the music box. She laughed so beautifully and contagiously that it was impossible not to feel calm.

I listened to the recording hundreds of times until it broke down completely. Dad couldn't fix it anymore.

Today, after so many years, when sadness tears the flesh off of me with its bare hands, I close my eyes. But I don't cry.

I'm protected by that child's laughter, which I still hear—the laughter in the box.

Divorce, Hatred, and Rebirth

David M. Oancea

Why would I choose to write about the most painful period of my life? I've come to realize that a pain point is often the only thing that has the potential to motivate me to decide to change for the better. Just like pain is necessary to build muscle and develop physical fitness, pain is necessary to build character and correct course.

No matter how much I wanted my life to follow a linear path of high school, college, upper-level degrees, solid career, marriage and family, and comfortable retirement, I discovered early on that the best plans must adapt to circumstances outside my control.

After I married the woman I had hoped would be my life partner, and we started a family, I believed that I had crossed one of the most important thresholds in life. After ten years, tragedy struck suddenly, unexpectedly, and with finality. The next two and a half years of divorce proceedings, evaluations, counseling, financial hardship, estrangement, and emotional suffering took their toll on me, my daughter, and my family members.

For quite some time, I felt hatred toward my former wife and all those who helped initiate the break-up of a marriage, a family, and the flow of life as I knew it.

Faith, prayers, the support of relatives and friends, counseling, and the passage of time gave me a new and healthier perspective. I realized that any hatred I carried in my heart and mind only hurt me. I came to understand that this devastating experience that tore up my life as I knew it was necessary. Only then could I rebuild it on a new foundation, repair relationships that had suffered in the process, and experience a kind of rebirth. It has taken several years to come to terms with these most unhappy events. I learned a lot about myself in the process and am thankful to God for this opportunity and his presence during the lowest and most difficult periods.

I would not wish on anyone the kind of crisis or challenge that I experienced. However, I believe that everyone must keep in mind that the word "crisis" in the Chinese language may be very instructive. It is composed of two characters: one meaning danger and the other, opportunity.

Worship, Not Entertainment

Cornel Todeasa

Our participation in the life of the Church enriches us in many ways. For example, through the readings, the preaching, and the content of the hymns, holy learning takes place during the church's divine services. We also seek fellowship and engage in acts of charity with the other church members. However, we are primarily gathered in the Body of Christ, the Church, to seek our salvation and to give glory, thanks, and worship to our God.

But what do we mean by worship? In Luke 7:36-50, we read the story of a time when Jesus was a guest in the house of a Pharisee. His host was a cultured man who would surely have known how to honor an important guest, but he didn't even offer Him the minimum traditional hospitality — water to clean the dust from his feet.

While Jesus was in the Pharisee's home, a sinful woman entered and threw herself at the feet of Jesus. She, not the Pharisee, treated Jesus as an honored and most welcomed guest. She "washed His feet with her tears" (v. 38).

There is a sharp contrast, noticed by the Lord Himself, between the outward religion of the Pharisee and the heartfelt adoration of the sinful woman. The Pharisee is seen as merely entertaining Jesus, while the sinful woman truly adored and worshiped Him.

Who are we like? Do we, like the Pharisee, take Christ for granted and fail to respond to Him with true hospitality? Or are we like the sinful woman? Do we offer to Our Lord only the riches of our possessions, or do we offer "ourselves and our whole life" to Him?

We are presented with the example of the sinful woman to learn about repentance, humility, and our love for God. The sinful woman teaches us that we are not to entertain Jesus but instead, to worship Him. Our church, which maintains the truth received from the Apostles, is not a church for merely entertaining Jesus and His teaching. It is the holy place where Jesus and our God in the Holy Trinity are worshiped and glorified.

There might indeed be other places where we can learn about God: in Bible Study groups, from books in the privacy of our homes, and even in front of the television set. But there is only one place where we can truly worship God, and that is in His Church.

The Circle of Life

Lori Foley-Jacquez

In a rush to get my first grader out of the house and to school on time, he happened to look out our backyard window as we headed out and noticed a grasshopper in our pool. The insect was struggling to stay afloat. My son asked if he could go help it and put it somewhere "safe." As he rushed out, running to save his newfound friend, he gently scooped him out of the water and looked around the backyard for a place to settle on. I was at the back door, reminding him that we needed to get going and to please find a home quickly. He decided to place his friend on our wall, which was covered by a low-hanging tree, where, in my son's exact words, "The grasshopper could dry off and be safe!" As my son walked towards me to leave, he looked up and exclaimed, "It's not the right place for him; I don't think he will be safe!" He ran back and brought his friend to me.

I told my sweet son, "We need to get going, and this grasshopper now looks like he is dry and can fly; let's let him try to find his own safe place, where he would like to settle in for the morning!" This six-year-old looked at me in a way I'll never forget how he trusted the suggestion but was not sure it would work.

I leaned over, cupped my son's tiny hand from below, and said, "On the count of three, we will raise up your hand with a quick, swift movement and throw him into the air; he will then fly on. His own!" I was optimistic that this technique would work perfectly and, more importantly, quickly! We counted to three, and with one swift movement, my son's hand went up; the grasshopper took off and started flying as we predicted. We both had smiles instantly on our faces!

Except, what we didn't know, was as the grasshopper took flight, a hungry bird came out from the tree and instantly scooped up the grasshopper! My son yelled, "Noooooo!" and my heart dropped into an invisible abyss as to what just happened! I immediately knelt and hugged my son, looked him in the eyes, and said, "You just witnessed the Circle of Life, son, and that bird, thank you for his breakfast!".

Katerina

Eugen V. Rosu

I called her last week to wish her a "Happy Birthday." She was pleasantly surprised to hear from me. When I asked her how are things going in her life, her answer became an avalanche of words of joy and excitement. She jumped from one subject to another because she wanted to tell me everything about her new life.

I met Katerina years ago when I visited her in her hospital bed. She lay in bed crying. I waited for her to get her composure back. While calling, she asked me to wait for her because she wanted to talk to me. She began with her medical condition and then brought into the discussion her children, whom she missed greatly. The far distance between her stay and the children was devastating. She shared with me man things that were going on in her children's lives and that she wasn't a good mother to them because she was not there. Many guilty feelings are associated with her illness and her separation from her family. She told her story without interruption. At one point, she stopped and asked me if I was still listening to her. I smiled at her and affirmed that I was listening, and I repeated a few things back. Then, for the first time, I saw her smiling. She cleaned her eyes, looked at me, and said, *you probably think I am crazy*. We talked for a little while, and after that, when I was around, I stopped to see her. One day she told me how much she enjoyed photography. It was a eureka moment for me. I talked with the head nurse and managed to secure a camera for her to take pictures of the nurses working there and everything she saw outside.

One day I stopped to see her, and she showed me the pictures she had taken. It was almost like a new mother showing the picture of her new baby. We sat together, and she explained what each picture was about. While looking at the pictures, I saw her face shine; her smile flooded her whole being. Katerina, that was crying the first day we met, was gone. A new Katerina appeared. It was a Katerina full of life. A Katerina who wanted to get better faster and be again with her family. One weekend her husband came with the kids. She cried again, but this time were tears of joy. She invited me to meet her family. A caring husband and lovely kids.

Her curious eyes always looked to find something new. She was very curious to find out why I chose to become a priest. I was asked this question many times in my life. My answer was not to her liking, for she looked away and found another question. Then she looked at me and told me that she saw me in any other profession, yet I chose priesthood. That summer, we separated after my residency program, and soon after, she went home.

We remained in touch, and today, I listen to her voice full of joy and excitement about how fulfilled her children's lives are and how happy she is to be an excellent young grandmother. We both laughed. She told me how blessed she felt to have many people praying for her, encouraging her, and helping her find her purpose. She told me that she is amazed to know that she survived and lived longer than she thought and that she got to see her children grow and be fulfilled. For her, the whole journey with much pain, many tears, and countless operations, she is still around to tell her story. A story of courage. Story of fighting to overcome challenges. A story of love for the gift of life. "Happy Birthday, Katerina!"

I Wanted to Become a Priest...

Ronald Rock

I attended a Catholic grade school for six years. Attending Mass was mandatory for all students.

Sitting behind the class in the aisle seat was our ever-present Sister. She was an intimidating presence in her floor-length habit, a stern face framed by her headpiece. She sat with her knobby interlocked fingers in her lap. Her eyes spoke volumes when nodding her head wasn't enough. She brought the fear of God into us. No one dared cross her at Mass, in class, or anywhere.

So, it was always a welcoming relief when Father entered our classroom. The atmosphere of the class would change almost immediately. It always took a few seconds for Sister to acknowledge and accept the interruption. It was nice to experience his spirituality, presence, and wit away from the altar. He had a calm, nurturing, and frequently humorous presence. He was someone who could bring a smile, as forced as it may have been for Sister to bring on. He was a good man in my book.

It was then that I thought the priesthood might be my calling. I became an acolyte at my first opportunity and served as many Masses as I could. I signed up for weddings, funerals, and anything else the parish needed.

Eventually, I attended the seminary.

We were housed in dormitories resembling military barracks. Classes were enjoyable. The instructors were accommodating and reminded me of our priests and Monsignor back home. I felt my future was on the right track.

I was welcomed, although I still felt out of place and distanced from my fellow seminarians. I struggled to put the finger on why I felt this way.

Discussions with counselors were unsuccessful. Self-reflection was an exercise in futility. Even prayer did not help, or I did not see it. After countless nights of prayer in search of direction, I realized that serving God as a priest was not my calling.

I made a very difficult decision to leave the seminary to seek another career in service. I knew in my heart it was the right move.

As 1 Peter 4:10 states, "As each one has received a special gift, employ it in serving one another as good stewards of the multifaceted grace of God." I am now retired after a successful career of forty-seven years in healthcare, and I thank God for His guidance and blessings.

Why Not!

Emilian-Ciprian Ene

My wife, Silvi, had been planning with several friends of ours for a few days to surprise me for my birthday. Silvi tells me two days in advance that I have to wake her up early. She usually wakes up later. I was amazed and told her I was helping her.

On Saturday morning, I wake her up, thinking I can still sleep. She told me that I had to get up now because a friend of ours wanted to surprise us, and we had to be in his car by seven. We drove past places I knew very well. I realized that we wouldn't be fishing, but I still didn't know what was coming. I was like a child waiting for a gift, but I didn't know what it was.

My wife introduced me to a woman. The lady asked me if I had ever jumped from 4000 meters. Then, I burst out laughing with realization. I hadn't realized what was coming even though I was on an airfield where only parachute jumps are made and where I had jumped five years ago. I got on the plane.

During my first experience, when the parachute opened, I fainted. Because of that, I could not enjoy the whole experience. On the plane, I had felt fear.

When the door to this plane opened, I felt terror, but I told the instructor, "I'm scared, but I'm jumping anyway!" The instructor motioned for me to sit on the edge of the plane, and I jumped.

Wow! I felt every moment of the jump. The concept of time no longer existed for me in those moments, as if everything was happening in another time.

This time I even managed to drive the parachute a little and pay attention to the strings, to how the parachute was above us. It was a huge joy that I was in control of, even for a little bit. I managed to enjoy the new experience fully this time.

After taking the equipment off me, I screamed with joy and jumped like a child.

Overcoming Fear

Luminita-Elena Stoenescu

One snowy winter, we decided to go to the mountains and learn to ski. Wanting to go somewhere new, we chose the resort of Kopaonik in Serbia. Kopaonik has 25 ski slopes. There were two adults and two children.

The road trip was pleasant. We quickly found an experienced instructor, and, for four days, he trained us with the utmost seriousness. At first, everything was like child's play. But, as it got harder, I could not keep my balance. The falls were more frequent, so I climbed the track for beginners. Although I thought about the instructor's advice, I could not keep my balance for a long time. When I picked up speed, I panicked and would hit the ground.

I felt that I could not continue, even though I saw hundreds of people skiing with ease. I had to do something; otherwise, fear would take over me. While my husband and children relaxed on the playground, I took the ski lift to the Blue Slope, where people seemed to be flying down the slope. It did not seem like a place for beginners like me, but I dared. We reached the top of the hill. Looking down, I thought now was the time to overcome my fear. I said out loud, "God help me!" I took a deep breath and let go.

My heart was pounding. I could see young and experienced skiers quickly overtaking me on both sides. I reached the bottom of the slope without losing my balance! The fear disappeared. I was glad that I managed to overcome a moment of fear that seemed to overwhelm me. When I told the instructor that I had let go of my fears on the Blue Slope, he was amazed by my courage and exclaimed, "You are crazy, and you deserve a diploma for that!"

I firmly believe that we must have incredible audacity to help us overcome our limits, but as the old Latin proverb says, "Nihil sine Deo."

Serenity

Ioan Rosu

On a Sunday afternoon, I went with my aunt to a sheepfold near the village where my grandmother lives to visit the sheepfold and see how sheep cheese is made.

Before reaching the sheepfold, we passed through a forest with towering trees that formed a thick shadow over the road.

I was excited to see what a sheepfold looks like and how to prepare sheep's cheese at the stable.

Once we reached the sheepfold, we sat in the shade of an old oak tree and enjoyed the fresh air. The sheep were grazing nearby, and we listened to the murmur they made as they ate the green grass. It was a silence hard to describe. The sheep grazed as if on a well-established rule, and they moved in a compact group like a giant lawnmower. Toward evening, the shepherd mined the canvas to the sheepfold, where, together with the dog, they would milk them.

When the milking was over, I curiously asked the shepherd how to make delicious sheep's cheese. He explained to me how to prepare the milk, and then the product, and how the thicker milk product is put in a gauze drain.

While he told me about the whole cheese-making process, I tasted a piece on the house as they gave us as a welcome sign.

The Badger—A Winter Story

Eugen V. Rosu

During the winter months, women got together to help each other prepare wool for weaving. They would go from one woman's house to another to spin the yarn, then get it in clews.

As children, we helped. We had to keep our arms in an oval shape to help prepare the wool. We had to move our arms to keep up with the women preparing the wool. After a while, our shoulders would become numb and our moves irregular. At that point, the wool around our arms was no longer perfectly stretched.

These gatherings were special occasions where the women shared recipes and sang folk songs and religious hymns. Around Christmas, we sang carols and shared stories. The host would always have something prepared for all to eat, though the other women would bring something special to share like apples, walnuts, savory apple pies, and quinces baked in the oven. No one had a television. There were no game gadgets.

We read books and listen to the women's stories. Some of the stories were funny. Others were spooky. And there were riddles! One woman, in particular, seemed to be an encyclopedia of riddles. Every time we met, she had new ones without repeating any.

One story stuck with me over the many years. It was about men going into the forest to hunt badgers. The men would set fire at the entrance to get the badgers out of their dens, and smoke made the beasts come out. One day, one man thought he could enter a little deeper in the hole to set the fire so the smoke would work faster. He got deeper and deeper, neglecting the calls of his fellow hunters. When he tried to get out, his sheepskin coat formed a thick and stubborn ring around his waist, and he no longer could leave the den. His comrades tried to get him out but to no avail. In the Spring, people hiking in the forest found pieces of the man's coat.

As we went back home, I held my mother's hand very tight. The moon lit up the sky, and the frozen snow made funny noises under our feet. I still remember the trembling.

Silvia

Dana Fodor Mateescu

ilvia Olimpia Otilia Iolanda Magdalena Mateescu, aka Ciucureta. She was my puppy. A German Shepherd. She would have turned four in September.

I would look out the window of the back door and wait for her ears to appear. She always held a piece of wood in her mouth.

Now, I know she's not coming back. She cannot come back. My Ciucureta is gone. I found her dead in the courtyard on Friday, June 11. Stiff, with her mouth clenched and eyes open. She had vomited blood. She died in agony but made no sound.

On that day, I drank my coffee on the terrace and noticed that she did not appear. She usually sat with me and kissed me on my right hand as I carried the cup to my lips. But she hadn't come that morning.

"Where's Ciucureta?" Răzvan asked me.

"She will be here soon," I told him, but it never crossed my mind that something might happen. He went to look for her. Then, I heard him scream, "Silvia! Ciucureta! SILVIAAAAAAAAAAA!" He called for me.

The blood in my head stopped. Death was hidden in his voice. I don't know how I got to the front of the house. I threw myself on her and cried like for my mother. Why did she die? She wasn't sick.

She was cheerful, agile, and beautiful. She had gone on a walk with Andrei in the evening.

"Mother, Silvia didn't want to leave the yard. She normally could wait to leave. I went to the store and back without her," my child told me.

I called the vet. I sent her a picture of Silvia as I found her. The vet suspected intoxication. She must have eaten something toxic." *Poison! Poison? When? How?* She never took anything from the floor. Had she swallowed rat poison? Had she eaten a mouse? We will never know.

I miss her, I see her red collar, and I feel faint. I look for her to feed her, and then I remember that she's gone. Today, when I was sweeping the fallen mulberries off the floor, I waited for her to come and eat. I can hear her barking, and I can still smell her.

But now she's gone.

It's raining outside. Everything makes me think of Silvia—the grass, the windows, the terrace, and the mulberries that she liked so much.

Goodbye, my little tassel! Forgive me for everything! You made my life more beautiful.

The Game That Mirrors Life

David M. Oancea

My parents encouraged my siblings and me to do well in school, engage in clubs and activities, learn to play a musical instrument, and participate in various sports. As a youngster, I tried various organized sports: tee-ball, baseball, basketball, football, ping-pong, and tennis. Of all the sports, racquet sports were what I loved most. I could play ping-pong for hours in the basement with my brothers and friends. I enjoyed the exhilaration of hitting a ball, directing its trajectory, and the rush of competition.

I don't know when I caught the "tennis bug," but one of the activities I enjoyed most was hitting a tennis ball in the summertime for hours against a brick wall at the local park. When I started playing tennis competitively on an actual court, I fell in love with the challenges of the sport. As my skills increased and I had the opportunity to observe professionals on television and accomplished players in person, I began to see that there are other dimensions beyond the physical.

Attitude and mental focus are key to playing the game successfully. Hitting a spinning ball that moves at various speeds and is influenced by the environment requires concentration, athletic ability, and balanced movement.

I began to realize that competition magnified my own as well as my opponent's personality and character. Good and not-so-good qualities come to the surface during intense competition. Observing behavior on the court became a lesson in psychology. I also learned how to deal with opponents who consistently made bad line calls and attempted to cheat to win a match.

There was a period in my life when I stopped playing tennis due to work and family responsibilities. During that period, my personal life hit its lowest point. Once I began playing again, the game brought focus, fitness, joy, and balance back into my life.

Time and again, this challenging yet simple game has made me realize that it mirrors life. If I pay attention, the way I play the game and how I react in the heat of competition provides a snapshot of my physical, emotional, intellectual, and spiritual state in real-time.

Being On Time

Cornel Todeasa

Once, I was a guest at a Retiree's Club luncheon scheduled for 12:30 at the church. Everybody was on time or early. We said the prayer at 12:30, and immediately, the lunch was served. I was so impressed with their punctuality that I remarked, "I'm amazed that we can be on time for a lunch, but not for the Divine Liturgy."

"We are on time for lunch because we are hungry," someone replied, which drew some laughter. Why don't we have such hunger and thirst for the holy things? "Blessed are those who hunger and thirst for righteousness, for they shall be filled," the Lord says in His Sermon on the Mount (Matthew 5:6).

If we had pangs of hunger and a deep thirst for spiritual food and drink, we would be on time for Sunday services in anticipation of receiving everlasting food and living drink from God. The Church would be full even before the priest announced the beginning of the Great Banquet, the Divine Liturgy.

As illustrated in the parable of the Great Supper (Luke 14:15-24), the Divine Liturgy is the spiritual banquet offered by the Father and in which the Son gives of Himself in Holy Communion for the forgiveness of our sins and everlasting life.

Many times, the best opportunity to feed our souls is on Sunday at the Divine Liturgy. Coming late, or not coming at all, to the Divine Liturgy deprives our souls of spiritual sustenance. Through our negligence, we allow them to starve, even unto death. Therefore, "with the fear of God, with faith and with love, draw near," always and on time to the Divine Liturgy, and partake of the heavenly banquet.

Paleontologist

Eugen V. Rosu

My little girl, before attending preschool, watched a show about the dinosaurs. At the end of each episode, the show featured a paleontologist who offered more details about one dinosaur. There were much statistical data about the size of the ancient creature, what it ate, and some behavior. During the time the show aired, my daughter stood still in front of the television. The whole universe stopped. Nothing moved. Her favorite dinosaurs: triceratops, velociraptor, t-rex, and the pterodactyl, were carefully placed on the table in front of the television. Sometimes she held them.

Once the show was over, with the live intervention of the scientist, she declared to us that she wanted to become a paleontologist. Since the dinosaurs were her dolls, for she had only two dolls, mainly at the bottom of a toy box, my wife and I encouraged her to become a paleontologist. She was so happy about her future, and to convince us, she immediately shared with us, mostly with me, about her learnings. I had to focus and look straight at her. If I moved my head a little, she grabbed my head in her palms and turned me around to look at her. She was able to repeat almost every detail she learned about the dinosaur presented. Even today, after many years, she still remembers the facts about her friends, the dinosaurs.

The time came for her to go to preschool. We dropped her off in the morning. After I had called two times in the morning and once in the early afternoon to ask how my dear daughter was doing, it finally came the time to go to pick her up from school. I was greeted by her teacher, who had a big smile on her face and told me that my baby said to her that she wanted to become a paleontologist. The teacher was amazed that her new student could pronounce a long and complicated word and did it. I explained to her the source of inspiration for my little girl's career. The teacher was impressed, but she still could not believe that a three-year-old could pronounce a hard word, so clearly. Since then, my offspring changed her focus on becoming a zoologist.

Of The Emigrant

Em Sava

Some of the greatest joys of the emigrant are those in which he waits for his parents and relatives to visit. In addition to the happiness of a reunion with loved ones, the emigrant relives his beginning. As every beginning is charming, new life in a foreign country is like a love story. People say that the first part of living in a new land is somewhat of a honeymoon for the emigrant.

At that time, it is poetry. You marvel at everything new, and you have the joy of discovery. It is the adventure and the promise of the chance of a new life. You feel like you have enormous wings. Then, you come face to face with the prose of reality, the difficulties of the job, the installments at home, the bills, the cold and the heat, the language barrier, and other common challenges.

Every October, we felt happy when our parents would visit and stay with us for several months. They had grown accustomed to spending the winter with us and leaving after the Easter holidays. They were present for some small and big events in our new life. They came for years, allowing us the joy of pampering them and walking them across Canada.

We shared beautiful memories that bloomed like cherry blossoms in the Spring. We did this for years until my father decided not to fly because of his health. One day, he decided to fly. But this time, it wasn't on a plane, but with his soul, in other dimensions, away from us.

We are the sum of our memories. In the many years we spent together, I felt blessed to have them for my winters. They enjoyed our beautiful life here, the home we have built. In the end, man sanctifies the place. My father often said to me, "you took my face around the world"—because I wear his features like a holiday dress.

A Wave of Vain Questions

Angelina Nădejde

If, on rainy mornings,
I brought you a sun,
would you love me?

If, by chance,
there were poppies on the hills
I would steal them out of purity,
and, like jasmine flowers,
I could wash away your make-up,
Would I have you?

Asleep in tears
the proudest of them,
I beg for an arm of stars,
to weave you a wreath,
would we be together?

If I were alone in a
lighthouse on the shore, in a storm,
I would save myself to see your face,
in the light, in the morning

And reinventing destinies,
would you love me, then?

If both my hands,
not knowing what time was,
painted your face on the vault
and, out of tears and verse,
sculpt a universe for you,
would I be your chosen one?

I would build myself in you
just to know you're with me.
I don't expect clear answers,
that I know them already
hurts.

Leave me doors ajar,
at least in your dreams,
in the light to carry me
to be with you.

Guilt Versus Gratitude

Ronald Rock

I cannot imagine any person not having been affected by the pandemic. Personally, I have been blessed with good health, and my recent retirement has left me financially secure. Why is it then that I feel so guilty about family and friends who have not been as fortunate?

You need only to look at some news feeds to realize the entire world is suffering. Globally, people are not only suffering through the pandemic. There are wars, floods, fires, and economic and personal hardships compounding matters.

Why do I continue to feel guilty about the security in my life? Is it survivor's guilt? Survivor's guilt is a feeling of guilt in people who have survived a life-threatening event when others have died. It is a thought that creeps into the minds of survivors. *Perhaps I could have done more to save them.*

As a healthcare provider, I'm used to fixing things. When I cannot, there is a feeling of frustration, failure, and disappointment. I'm learning that I cannot always fix other people's situations, and I should not feel guilty about mine. The best I can do is to acknowledge their circumstances and offer support as best I can. It is a personal struggle, however, not to get more involved.

I must feel gratitude, not guilt, for my family, my home, and my financial security. I must feel grateful for being able to enjoy life's countless simple pleasures. After all, if I cannot advocate for myself, how will I be able to advocate for others?

There should be no reason to feel guilty. I know life will throw me curveballs as well. I know the world won't resolve its issues any time soon. I will continue to learn how to best support those suffering whenever and wherever I can without trying to fix them.

I can only hope and pray for the world to become a better place. In the meantime, I will be grateful for what I have and thank God for everything.

But Watch for the Blind Spot

Cornel Todeasa

In our prayers, we ask God to "forgive our voluntary and involuntary trespasses, in word and indeed, in knowledge and in ignorance."

We are inclined to think that our involuntary trespasses, those committed in ignorance, are less sinful than those committed voluntarily and with knowledge. When we sin with knowledge, don't we bear more personal responsibility? Should doing something wrong in ignorance even be considered a sin?

I found an answer when I pondered the idea of a car's blind spot. Learning to drive, I was constantly reminded to "watch for the blind spot." They're found on either side of a car, areas that cannot be seen in any mirror, so we must turn our heads to watch for them. We're not exonerated from any accident that might happen because we haven't watched for the blind spots. On the contrary, we must accept the consequences.

Perhaps associating the sins committed in ignorance with accidents resulting from ignoring the blind spots in our cars is a far-fetched idea. In my mind, however, they are similar. We commit sins of ignorance because we do not pay attention to unseen troubled spots of our character, the hidden shadows of our souls, and our moral "blind spots."

These sins are more dangerous for our salvation. Arising from our tarnished nature or bad habits, they do not appear to us as sins anymore but as normal acts. We tend to dismiss them from the start. We might not even confess these sins. If we do confess them, we must try to understand their roots or causes, or we will fail to find spiritual medicine for our souls.

The sins of ignorance should not be ignored. When they surface in our lives, we must react just as we do at a railroad crossing. Stop. Look into our souls, to the left and the right. Try to see and understand the source of these sins. A good confessor can help us.

But let us not ignore these sins because if they are ignored and not spiritually treated, they will grow. Then, one day we will not see the heavy train coming straight at us seemingly "out of nowhere," from our blind spot, endangering our salvation.

Don Calistru

Eugen V. Rosu

He was known as Don Calistru. A revered and a bit feared teacher. He was when many generations learned how to untie the mysteries of a novel or to understand a specific genre influenced by historical circumstances. He was the only high school teacher who walked into the classroom without books, notes, or papers. The only thing he brought with him was the grade class note. Everything was in his head and his heart.

It was the time in the ninth grade when we were studying the old Romanian literature. As was the case everywhere in Europe, the first printed books were the Bible and many church-related books. The teacher told us about the importance of printed books and the beauty of the language as it was in the early 16th century. As the class unfolded, one classmate asked a question about the validity of the Bible. To support his interest, he used a text from a book published by the political propaganda of the Communist Party. Such books were published every other month to undermine anything that had a stand against the communist doctrine. In those books, the authors used short verses from the Bible, or sometimes one or two words, to make their point against Church and faith. Other times the authors made use of classic Romanian literature for the same purpose of making the communist teachings stronger.

Once my classmate finished his question, Don Calistru gave his answer. That was the only time I saw him furious. His response was short but full of insight. He told us that if we want to know what the Bible says, we should read the Bible and not take any teachings from those "garbage books."

The last words were strong enough to have him pay a visit to the secret police, or perhaps he was invited there. For me, that was a point of pushed curiosity to find and read a Bible. Bibles were not available in every bookstore. These books were rare items to find, and if you wanted one, you needed to know somebody who, which in turn, knew somebody. My Romanian language teacher, Don Calistru, and my priest were the people who had a powerful influence on my decision to pursue theological studies. His demeanor made a significant impact on me, and I am sure in many other students' lives.

Joe's Bakery

Eugen V. Rosu

I am sure that we all have stopped at some point to ask for directions. Of course, the person giving directions, a local, can offer accurate information.

I needed some clarification on the directions I had written on a piece of paper. The area was a residential one with a great deal of natural landscape. Luckily, a local bar, the only business in the area, opened early that morning. The four men inside were happy to assist. The bartender immediately explained that I needed to drive through three more stoplights and make a right turn at Joe's Bakery. The other men confirmed it, and I was happy knowing that I would be on time for my appointment.

I drove according to the given directions through three stoplights, and then I was on the look for Joe's Bakery. I passed the fourth and the fifth stoplight and did not see the bakery. I went to another establishment to ask for directions and clarification on where the major landmark was. The lady at the counter looked at me and said, "You are not from here!" *Well, only visitors can ask for directions,* I thought.

As soon as she continued, I learned that not being from there had a different meaning. She explained that Joe's Bakery closed 25 years ago, that two other businesses used the place, and that the space had been empty for about five years. Only then was it clear to me what she meant by "you are not from here."

Local people knew Joe's Bakery as a landmark, which was a thriving family business for more than 50 years. A few people remembered the two stores after because they stayed for a very short time and were unsuccessful. The baker's family was part of the neighborhood, and all the neighbors ordered their cakes from them and, occasionally, the kids would get a little treat from Joe. It was a unified community.

Joe's Bakery became such a landmark in people's minds, even though the ones who ran the bakery were no longer among the living. The memory of those excellent and funny years was vivid for the community. No one could forget Joe's treats. The whole neighborhood was a big family.

Grateful Beyond Words

Ronald Rock

We have all heard the idea of someone seeing life flash before them in a life-threatening moment. Such was the case as I stared down the barrel of a handgun in a patient's room.

My partner and I were called to a patient's room. Upon our arrival, we sat the patient down on the couch. My partner grabbed the clipboard as I sat down on the other end of the couch to begin the paperwork. Once done, I stood up to perform the physical examination. I opened the medical kit and grabbed the blood pressure cuff.

Unbeknownst to my partner or me, as our backs were momentarily turned, our patient had reached down between the couch cushions and armrest to grab a gun.

As I approached to take his blood pressure, I saw the barrel pointed directly at me. It was out of sight from my partner. I could see the hollow-point bullets in the cylinder, the hammer cocked, and his finger on the trigger. Once my partner saw the gun, he knew any sudden movement would startle the patient. I could see the fear and helplessness in his eyes.

I can only imagine what he saw in mine.

At that moment, I locked eyes with the patient hoping not to become a casualty myself. I watched him squeeze the trigger as my family and entire life simultaneously and instantaneously flashed before my eyes.

Moving forward, I reached out towards the gun. Our heads collided, and the gun exploded by my ear. At that instant, I was praying for a miracle. I questioned if I was going to live or die. I had hoped my life was worthy of eternal salvation. I thanked God and took a breath as I watched the bullet shift its trajectory as if in slow motion.

I wrestled the gun away as my partner quickly subdued him. Standing in front of our patient with his gun safely at my side, I could now see the fear in his eyes. He knew how easily things could have ended if I didn't interrupt him, which I suspect is what prompted his pleas for forgiveness.

I have forgiven him. In fact, I feel indebted to him for showing me how precious life and my family are and, more importantly, how quickly they can be taken away without any warning or preparation.

Morits

Dana Fodor Mateescu

Morits left home every Monday
when the morning nursed the children of the night.
All the doors hurt.

He was carrying a piece of death in his sack,
sheep cheese and red onion
placed there by his wife,
that one, bitter as gray medicine.

Moriţs hated this color!
The shade of a perfect dead.

However, he loved his wife. Why not love her?
She was good. She styled herself. She ate poppy seeds,
and she talked until she fell asleep.

She made sure he always came home
like a thread-drawn doll,
like an ox,
or like a dog licking his sleeping place.

Morits was a golden man.
He only lied on Thursday.
His mouth was like black water
in which the fish wept with laughter.
Happiness enters through his eyes
to rot in his chest.

Be Still

Cornel Todeasa

Last year, Louisa, my wife, gave me a present. It was a garden plaque that read, "*Be still and know that I am,*" from Psalm 46:10. I hung it from a garden post and read it every time I entered the gate.

I wake up, as Elvis Presley once sang, "early in the morning while the dew is still on the roses." Being in the garden that early is divine. There is such a stillness that you can hear the voice of the Lord. I stand quietly, watching my plants grow and listening to their song of praise to God. Have you ever laid your head on the grass and listened to it grow, or do we do that only when we are young and still pure in our hearts?

The plants in my garden praise the Lord. With the green of their leaves, they glorify the Lord. With their growth, they witness Him. I place seeds in the ground, but God waters them. He gives them light, warmth, and air for growth. He shapes their flowers and brings their fruit to maturity. When the plants turn towards the light, they are growing towards God, looking for His face imprinted in the sunshine.

I wrote these words when I was still an active parish priest. Although I am now retired, I still strive to grow towards God only now from a paradise by the ocean. I still like to wake up early and walk with my wife on the beach. The ocean breeze caresses my face and blows my hair, as much as I have left, which keeps the heat of the summer down. The waves sing relaxing tunes. The pelicans patrol the waters, and the dolphins surface to take in air. Little sandpipers dig for food with their skinny beaks, running through the waves with their long legs.

When the sun rises, it permeates everything. It dissolves the darkness and opens the sky. It dips into the water, turning into every color in the spectrum. If in the garden I had the feeling of everything growing towards God, here, it is clear to me that everything arises from God every morning with the rising of the sun.

Wherever you are, walk slowly, look around, and feel the powerful presence of God's grace. Listen to God's words. *Be still and know that I am.* Immerse yourself in stillness, and you will know that God is. He was, He is, and He always shall be.

Wonders of Nature Through a Magnifying Glass

David M. Oancea

Summer gives me so much time to explore and follow my curious whims. One summer, when I was about ten years old, I lived in a small town in a fairly compact neighborhood with lots of kids. My bicycle took me everywhere, to the park down the street, to the creek, to friends' houses, to the library, to my grandmother's house.

We had a small yard, but the adjoining neighbors didn't mind if I wandered into their yards. I loved to explore outside and observe the world at my feet. A magnifying glass became one of my prized possessions. I could study grass, plants, leaves, rocks, and insects. I liked to collect lightning bugs after dark in a clear glass jar to create a natural lantern and observe how the bugs behaved.

At my grandmother's house, I enjoyed digging in the garden as deeply as I could, hoping to unearth some treasure or long-lost artifact. Milkweed grew in the fields on her property. The white, milky substance would drip from the plant when I pulled off the seed pod, and the intense scent held my attention. Tiny seeds attached to white feather-like sails filled the pod. When the pod dried and opened naturally, the wind caught the compacted seeds and drew out the feathery sails that carried the seeds far and wide.

I used my magnifying glass to observe the detail of the natural world, but I also liked to use it in other ways. Somehow, I discovered that capturing sunlight and focusing it on an object produced intense heat that erupted into flames very quickly. I started burning holes in leaves and catching dry grass on fire on the sidewalk.

We had large black ants on the walkways around our home, and I'd catch them behind their heads so that they couldn't bite me with their pincer-like mouths. I'm ashamed to admit that I would often capture one with each hand and bring them together to watch them fight with each other. Even worse, I experimented with the magnifying glass on them and other insects, killing them with the focused rays of the sun.

Self-directed learning in the school of nature during the summer months taught me lessons that I could not have learned in any classroom.

Not From A Distance

Cornel Todeasa

I like the song "From a Distance" as it is sung by Bette Midler. However, I have a problem with its theology. The song suggests a distant god who does not interact with us. This god is regarded as somehow aloof, at "a distance," almost cold to our needs, not interfering with us but merely watching over us.

This is not our God, not our true biblical God. Our God is not far away from us but with us. He knows us by name, as the shepherd knows his sheep. He walks with us, talks to us, listens to us, and feels with us. He is present in the people around us and in the beautiful world that surrounds us.

A hymn of the church referring to the events of Good Saturday confesses the ever-presence of our Lord, saying: As true God, fulfilling all things, O Christ, you were in the tomb in your body, in Hades with your soul, in Paradise with the thief, and on the throne together with the Father and the Holy Spirit: O You that are boundless. The boundless God is with us, and He is within us. St. Paul confesses this closeness with God by saying: "It is no longer I who live, but Christ who lives in me" (Galatians 2:20).

From another perspective, the song could be correct. There can be a distance between God and us, but it is not put there by Him. We set the "distance" between ourselves and God by our attachment to this world. We keep God out of our worldly surroundings. We exclude Him from our busy lives. Through our earthly and selfish actions, we shut Him out of the spiritual path leading to our hearts.

Even so, our Lord is still standing and knocking at the door of our souls. "If anyone hears My voice," says our Lord, "and opens the door, I will come into him..." (Revelation 3:20).

I like the song "From a Distance," but when I listen to it, in my mind, I always make a correction to that line of the song. I add a "not" before the word "from," so the song says: "Not from a distance," God is watching us. Indeed, God is very close to us. So, I pray that He will help me get rid of the earthly obstructions of my soul so He can come and always dwell within me.

Holidays

Em Sava

Christmas in Canada has never been like the Christmases I had growing up—not even when Canada became home. A few days before Christmas Eve, the phone vibrated in a friendly manner, helping me to exchange recipes. "Mom, how do you make stuffing for sarmale? Do I put sweet coconut in cookies? Salad . . . "

Both the phone and the computer began to vibrate with all our emotions. They became sensitive and fluid, almost human, in trying to get closer to their loved ones. Decks and boats were made. "See? We have so many applications . . . geography is an illusion." And I believed them. Of course, I believed them. Then, we lied. We told each other that it was the same even if the children didn't come with the carol.

Of course, they did not come because it was complicated. In Canada, the distances are great, and their parents would have needed to bring them. No more friends came to surprise us with the news of the Savior's birth at the windows. The distances were great. And how could it be Christmas without a slice of cake and a glass of wine or brandy?

The tree blinked proudly in the living room, and the computer captured on Skype the teary eyes of my mother and the sad smile of my father. We all mimicked the clash of glasses and sang carols on the phone. "How is winter with you?" Two dimensions were created like two stars in the sky with you and us with all the longing in them. The presents under the Christmas tree sat, waiting to be unwrapped. At the same time, Hruşcă filled the tricolor, and the living room was decorated with Christmas in Romanian.

We pushed our roots into the North American lands with our bare hands, and we intertwined the joy of each holiday in both Romanian and English as beautifully as we could. We have woven our customs and habits, food, and pleasures into a Babylon that we have become accustomed to, a Babylon to which we belong.

The Woman

Angelina Nădejde

When God created woman,
he gave her all that he could give,
the harmony of the body of a goddess
and the beauty of her soul.

God gave her a big heart
to envelope all the loves of the world,
love of husband, brother, parents,
but especially love for her child.

He left her the tenderness of a flower and the strength of a rock
which is not easily broken down.
He also gave her femininity,
to be the muse for artists,
painters, to be able to paint in colors
her cheeks flushed when she saw her lover,
joy or sadness in the eyes
and the charming smile.

To music, the nobility of the soul
to be in the songs of the troubadours of the world.
All this God put in the woman.

Grandmother Maria's Wisdom

Silvia Grigore

We know that God is Almighty and that the Devil has only the power that God allows, but for me, this was only clear after a tragic event.

My neighbors, Dana and Marian, died in a terrible car accident, leaving behind a nine-year-old girl named Cristina. Dana's mother was left to raise her granddaughter. Dana and Marian were poor, so neither Grandma Maria nor Cristina could have done otherwise. However, they never complained. They lived on the grandmother's pension and the girl's survivor's pension. When asked how she could raise the girl alone, the grandmother responded, "We have God."

The local priest took pity on them and appealed to the community so that all those who understood the pain of these two souls donated money. AA rich and arrogant man also heard the call. Being a man without compassion, he thought of making fun of the little girl and grandmother. He called an employee, made her buy food and beautiful clothes for the little girl, and then sent them to her. With the package the employee left on their doorstep, she also left a note that read, "I offer you this gift! Signed, The Devil."

What a joy for Grandma Maria to see that she has the opportunity to feed the little girl from the groceries in the basket, at least for a while. What a joy for the little girl that she will finally go to school with beautiful clothes.

The joy turned to sadness when they read the note! Who wouldn't be moved by Cristina's tears or the pain on Grandma's face?

Understanding that an evil man had made fun of them, the grandmother wondered how she could keep the package and make the little girl understand and accept. In her great wisdom, out of love for the little girl and out of trust in God, the grandmother said, "Let us receive the gift with joy, Cristina! Do you see how great God is? When He gives a command, even the Devil obeys it!"

A Wasted Life

Ronald Rock

Our ambulance was dispatched due to an unknown emergency. Upon arrival, a voice from the other side of the door commanded us to enter the apartment through the bathroom window. We squeezed our bodies through the small first-floor casement window. We were not certain of what to expect once we got inside. Once in, I carefully stuck my head into the hallway.

To my right, a young mother was sitting with her legs crossed. Nestled in her lap was her infant son. The child's lower body was snugly secured within his mother's legs. His chin was sticking out between her left index and middle finger, and his head was extended. His neck was exposed. It was then that I saw a long-serrated knife pressed up against it.

As a young paramedic, I had no experience in this type of crisis intervention. I retreated back into the bathroom to digest and share what I had seen. We quickly determined our next steps. The first was to notify the police. We knew time was of the essence. My partner offered to talk to her. However, the mother made it threateningly clear it was me she wanted to talk to.

I was terrified. I feared saying or doing the wrong thing. I knew enough not to make any quick movements or judgments about her actions. I lowered myself to the floor and began cautiously and fearfully edging toward her.

Even though only twenty minutes had passed, it felt like hours had gone by before the police arrived. I explained to the woman that the police would help her. Relieved at their presence, I retreated into the bathroom. Imagine the terror I felt when the mother called out, threatening to kill her infant if I didn't return into the hallway.

I prayed for guidance. Any suggestions the police had quickly evaporated as I reluctantly reentered the hallway. In the following thirty minutes, I thought I had gained her trust. I trembled with fear knowing the infant's life hung in the balance. We talked about her wants, needs, the innocence of her child, and her faith. She slowly relaxed her grip on the knife and the infant.

I was sitting next to her when she suddenly whispered, "I can't." I immediately reached for the knife as she tightened her grip on the infant and drew the knife across his neck.

I had failed, and it haunts me to this day.

Time to Relax

Elena Lupu

When they reached the cottage, they saw themselves in the middle of nowhere, surrounded only by the lazy sheep of the farm from which they rented the house. The only sounds were the rustle of the grass, the wind near the ears, the cows, and the sheep that seemed to have just now discovered the new patch of grass they had chosen with the utmost responsibility.

They seemed to be the only ones who did not belong in that landscape painted by some invisible hands of nature. After a moment of silence and a strong exhalation, the young people felt that they had made the best choice to spend their weekend in that place. Peace seemed to whisper to them from every leaf of the tree. And they felt it shiver down their spine. They did not expect such scenery. Their initial desire was to have fun for two evenings as for a week and leave the worries at home. But now, they seemed to want more. They wanted to feel inside the silence in which they had been drowning for tens of minutes.

So, on that night, they remained outside. And what a good decision they made! They lay on the cold grass, slightly damp and facing the sky. The jokes did not take long to appear and were followed by the most normal pauses of silence. It could not have been otherwise. That evening the sky decided that the stars should shine brighter, the moon prouder, and the wind blow more smoothly. The young people felt as in a dream. They seemed to float, although the ground was supporting them. They saw dreams and hopes dancing in the air, although all they saw was a night sky. They saw signs and meanings, although what they saw were constellations they did not know by name or form.

As suddenly as it started, it ended. The sleep had quickly taken hold of them and sent all to bed more tired than they could have imagined. But there was something different. A feeling of fullness in their chests that they could not explain. It was as if they took too much air into their lungs, and the two organs did not know how to cope and what to do with it. And with that state of mind, they went to bed and went to sleep. It's no secret that they woke up more rested and relaxed with an ashier smile on their faces; they woke up with a feeling of serenity that seemed to embarrass them to talk about the fear of running away again from the chaos of their home. But for now, they were not running anywhere because they had to stay one more night.

Linden Flowers

Eugen V. Rosu

The park looks like a botanical garden with flowers everywhere, and the myriads of fragrances enchant the people. A full pallet of colors is displayed in the park, and in some places, the colors seem to follow a specific pattern, which fools the eye when they vanish in a different color.

The roses open their arms and offer their beautiful red, white, yellow, and burgundy flowers. That dark red petal of the rose, which has a distinctive perfume, somehow controls the area's fragrance. The pansies offer their multicolor beauty with their discreet aroma.

The tulips are nicely aligned behind the pansies and seem to enjoy the bouquet from their lower sitting friends, in return offering their gracious looks waving in the calm wind like ballerinas.

Above all this spectacle of beauty and aroma stand the linden flowers. The tree, an old one, spread its branches generously to cover as much space as possible. From that height, the scent is carried around by the wings of the wind, at times dominating the whole area. The busy bees harvest the pollen from their wide-open flowers to prepare the light and delicious honey. That honey has a light-toned color that is easy to see through and is not as thick as it is from wildflowers.

When they no longer have pollen or their fragrance, these flowers make a stand in the park and fall in a swirl as mini-helicopters. As they fall, the flowers settle in the hair of the two lovers standing underneath the tree.

Nature shares its love with the people who admire it and take care of it. It is an intertwining of love and respect for one another. These flowers maintain their memorable fragrance in the journal of a young woman and in the memory of all those who enjoy them.

A Voice to Remember

Eugen V. Rosu

The crisp morning made all passersby move fast and go about their business. The coffee shops let the aroma of freshly brewed coffee and delicious pastries enchant the cold air of the burgh. The downtown stores were decorated for Christmas.

In the uproar of a cold December morning, there was something that made people stop in the street. Near the coffee shop, a blind man stood tall singing Christmas carols. Next to him, someone played a cassette player of the instrumental Christmas music.

At first, this looked casual. Many people sing Christmas carols around the city, but this singer was different. His deep bass voice warmed up the cold air on that block. The singing came out so naturally. It did not look like it took him any effort to sing so beautifully. His voice was strong enough to be heard by the entire block.

The songs were familiar to all passersby. Some of them even stopped to place money in the box in front of him. Others slowed to merely watch and absorb his divine voice. I remember a man with a leather coat, with two pagers clasped on his lapels, who strolled and murmured something about his beautiful singing. Others camped for a couple of minutes with their hot coffee in their hands to recharge with the magnificent voice, which sent an old message. The message of those Christmas carols became stronger because of the powerful voice.

Everything changed. People were not in such a hurry.

Music is a piece of art that makes people see their surroundings differently. Music unites people, even if only for a few minutes. I hope that the man could see the faces of the people who stopped to listen to him. He shared his divine gift with us all, and all received the blessing of his marvelous voice.

December

Asma Nooruddin

To provide some context about my background, I should mention my parents. Before the Bangladesh Liberation War, my father worked as a diplomat for the Pakistan Embassy. After his homeland gained independence, he was appointed as the chargé d'affaire of the Bangladesh Embassy and assumed his post in Afghanistan. Therefore, my early childhood was spent in the capital city of Kabul.

In December of 1975, a few months after returning from our vacation in Bangladesh, we received news about my maternal grandfather's worsening condition. My mother began to pray for his well-being. The following day, another telegram arrived, letting us know he had passed away.

My mother, stricken with grief, lay on her bed and wept. All of her friends came over to offer their condolences, but I was too little to understand why so many aunties were visiting at once. My older brother, who was eleven at the time, was far more perceptive.

He quickly brought his two younger sisters into his room, which was usually off-limits to us. There, he built a makeshift airplane out of the bed, a chair, and a wooden carom board. He placed me on the mattress and took a seat in the chair. Suddenly, he was a pilot, and I was his passenger. Meanwhile, my older sister acted as the flight attendant, serving us the snacks she had at her disposal. Since our recent trip to Bangladesh was fresh in our minds, it was easy to imagine the scene and play along.

I'm sure my mother appreciated the chance to quietly mourn her loss while her son watched for his sisters. While she yearned for her father, I yearned for my playmates. I would often imagine booking an entire plane for the cousins I had met in Bangladesh. I would bring them all to my home so that we would be together forever. It didn't occur to me that if my cousins were to settle down in Afghanistan, they would also miss those they would have to leave behind.

As an adult, I can finally recognize the feelings my mother must have carried inside of her. After all these years, I understand the longing of someone who has been separated from their loved ones, first by distance and then by death.

Where a plane ride once connected them, imagination must now suffice.

Don't Be Surprised!

Em Sava

We emigrated on a splendid spring day at the end of April, with the lilac ripe in purple and white flowers, with tricolor perfumes. It was bittersweet because we were leaving. Not nearby, but precisely eight thousand kilometers away, to a distant country. It was like a fairy tale overseas and across lands. And we went because that is how it was probably written for us.

Arriving in North America, I was amazed, among other things, by how people dressed. I had left behind an amazingly hot Romania to reach a country just coming out of winter.

I was cold. I was wearing my thick coat, while the locals were in shorts and T-shirts. I looked at them with eyes out of orbit like a snail without understanding what kind of skin these people have. They rejoiced. It was their way of celebrating and encouraging the coming of Spring. Winter had just left, and they, fed up with their thick clothes, hurried, even if they were a little cold blue, to throw off their warm clothes.

I got used to their habits in time, but I stuck with mine. My Romanian skin is thin and does not get along well with excessive heat or the biting cold. I learned not to be surprised. It is a cultural Babylon, a country that welcomes everyone regardless of color, creed, or custom. It is a permissive society that does not judge, does not put labels, and perhaps that is why life is better here because it all starts with the mentality.

It has been a wonderful experience, from the friendly greeting to the conversation about the weather, from the eagerness to get in the neighbor's pot and look over the fence to jumping to the aid of anyone—no matter a friend or stranger. In twenty years of living in Canada, I have been through many situations, both in the sun and shade. Some strangers were angels on earth. Because God works through people, we have to open the window of the soul.

We Live Virtually

Angelina Nădejde

I looked towards people
and I saw suffering,
sadness in their eyes, loneliness
and lack of love.

We pass carelessly
by lives handcuffed by helplessness
without having the strength
to talk to them.

We isolate ourselves in another world,
we write on our blogs about everything and anything
we advise in faith
and of living.

We have friends on Facebook,
we became as dependent on their likes
as of the caresses of those close to us.
We communicate and love them
without ever seeing them.
We share our feelings with them.

We embrace virtually,
but it gets harder and harder for us
to give a real hug
to those next to us.

Sometimes, with a single click,
someone can erase you
as if you never existed.

Every day, in the real world,
someone departs from us
poorer with a smile
a good word,
in love.

Mary and Martha In Us

Cornel Todeasa

Two sisters, Martha and Mary, had our Lord Jesus Christ as a guest in their home (Luke 10:38-42). They both loved our Lord. It cannot be said that one loved the Lord more than the other, but their expressions of love were so distinctly different that they had become paradigms for service and worship.

Martha was a down-to-earth person who cared more about life's immediate concerns. She was "distracted with much serving" (v. 40) and preoccupied with making the Lord's visit comfortable. Martha represents our earthly cares and tasks.

On the other hand, we have Mary, who, as soon as the Lord entered the house, sat down at His feet in adoration, listening to every word He spoke. Her actions exemplify an interest in spiritual things. Mary represents our heavenly concerns.

Burdened by her service, Martha complained and asked the Lord to order her sister to help her in the kitchen. Jesus replied, "Martha, Martha, you are worried and troubled about many things. But one thing is needful, and Mary chose that part, which will not be taken away from her" (Luke 10:40-42).

In saying this, the Lord is not rejecting Martha or her service to Him. He is, however, telling her that service alone is not sufficient. Our earthly cares are temporary and passing, but the heavenly cares are our treasures in Heaven — the worship and adoration of God, which were "the part" that Mary had chosen.

In our lives, we need both Martha and Mary. The two sisters complement one another. Martha and Mary model the inclinations of all people who struggle between these two dimensions of life, the temporary and the everlasting.

The Church— the Body of Christ — depends on both Martha *and* Mary, and the service of Martha must be complemented by the worship of Mary. Service can be given anywhere and at any time. But worship is the more specific work of the Church and should have precedence over service. In the Church, we sing praises to the Lord, we glorify Him, and we commune with Him in the Eucharist, which is the ultimate form of worship.

Now, do not try to figure out if you are a Martha or a Mary. The Lord wants us to be *both*. We must serve the Lord, as did Martha. At the same time, we must worship Him, as did Mary. In these secular times, it is easy to become Martha, but we must struggle to emulate Mary for the sake of our salvation!

Christmas Presence

David M Oancea

My daughter recently moved from Michigan to California. Through it all, we've remained connected, albeit at a distance. She's my only daughter, so she occupies a place in my heart that no one else can.

I've embarked on a new journey myself, by choice. This journey reflects my decision to be more authentic, more aware, and focused on how I feel about my life, its direction, and how I positively impact everyone around me, or not. I learned something about the "or not" part recently.

The present is all we have. I knew it on an intellectual level. I've even told others about this truth. I just haven't embraced it in my own life. I had to feel it on a "gut" level. That's the lesson my daughter taught me this Christmas.

You see, she invited me to visit for a few days. I told her that it would be great…BUT, certain projects at work and in my own personal life made it difficult for me to commit right away. "I'm not going to be able to come for Christmas," I told her after we had a protracted discussion about aspects of my own journey. I heard silence, then crying, and a hurt voice on the other end of the call. "I've felt like an afterthought after grandma and grandpa died," she said. I quickly responded that I didn't realize how much a visit from me meant and that I would reconsider. "I don't want a pity visit," she said.

"I'm sorry how our conversation ended," she said in a calm voice when she called a few days later. "It's really ok if you can't come. I understand." Before she called, my "gut" told me that visiting her was the right thing to do, that it was the opportunity to create a memory that I may not have again. I told her that I had bought a plane ticket and planned to visit. "Really, you're going to come?" she said excitedly. "Ok, then, we'll have Christmas dinner together. I just need to prepare some things. I returned some gifts I bought after you said you weren't coming."

That last sentence hit me hard. Only then did I realize how much my *presence* was valued above all the other things I had done for her to this point in her life. I told her: "Please don't get any presents. Let's make this Christmas only about being together."

That's the lesson my daughter taught me this Christmas. Christmas is about "presence," not "presents." The Son of God became man to be present with us, to show that God is a person and not some impersonal force.

Whatever your belief, being present to those around us, and especially our loved ones, is a practice that positively impacts our personal relationships, schools, workplaces, communities, and the whole world. "The present is all we have" is a universal truth. Have you learned that lesson yet?

Today

Asma Nooruddin

Every country has a treasure unique to its land and distinct from any other. In rugged and majestic Afghanistan, I was embraced by the most resilient and wholehearted people. In the beautiful and lush Pakistan, I relished the coziness and hospitality of a tender neighborhood. And in the familiar and bustling Bangladesh, I enjoyed the delightful and amusing company of family relations.

As I think back on my life, I am amazed by the blessings I have been given. Through these blessings, I could continue to serve those around me. Muhammad Ali once said, "Service to others is the rent you pay for your room here on earth."

After moving to Arizona, I was able to devote my energy to helping my community flourish. I also supported my husband as he worked to build a community center, which grew alongside my children. Now, it has become a bustling hub of activity far greater than us.

I know the love I received from my family and friends made it all possible. Although we try our best to make lasting contributions, our stay on earth is so brief. My one and only sister passed away this year, and her absence is deeply felt by all who knew her. She was like a second mother to me. While I can still hold onto her memory, I know it is time to move forward and celebrate her legacy.

The best I can give is through my children. They have gained diverse perspectives by introducing them to their heritage, encouraging their education, and surrounding them with excellent mentors. I can see how the three of them are becoming role models for the greater community, both in their homeland and abroad.

I could spend the rest of my days roaming the planet, reading books, and watching documentaries. I have only wandered so far, and there are still so many different cultures, communities, struggles, and triumphs to know and recognize. My stories may seem rather trivial compared to the breadth of human experiences. However, stories like these remind us of our common humanity and ought to be passed on to others. I am grateful for the opportunity to share mine, and I am forever thankful for the well-wishers and friends who have nurtured me in every land I've loved.

Canadian Christmas

Em Sava

The first Christmas in North America was strange. It was just the three of us. We had a plastic tree we adored because it was our first. It filled our desire to enjoy Christmas with our baby. He was always enthusiastic and told us, "Today is the most beautiful day of my life!" He was with his parents and discovering another world with us.

I am very close to my parents and have a visceral longing for home. It was kind of weird that Christmas was coming, and we were so far away. I still didn't feel at home. I enjoyed what I saw, the new experiences and feelings, and the people I knew, but in my soul, I was convinced that at some point, it would end, and we would return home. Sure, I was aware that I had opened and scattered that home like a puzzle game, but my soul could not accept that that place so dear to me, the apartment with four bright rooms in Cluj, existed only in my heart.

I had known enough Romanians because, at least at that time, the Canadian community embraced every newcomer. But each small community was developing an identity. Several Romanian churches were in the city, including two Orthodox ones, one for which I would teach Romanian a few years later. The people were kind and friendly, ready with their stories and advice on settling as an emigrant in Canada. Everyone has their own story and experience, and what suits one does not have to suit another.

We wrote our own story. The first Christmas was a timid copy of the Romanian one. Under the Christmas tree, we put most gifts for our boy to help him feel at home—something modest for us. I was just at the beginning of the road. With a festive smile, edged with some tears of longing, I cooked sarmale and cozonac to impregnate the Christmas house with a tricolor smell.

Where Do I Meet the Sacred?

Ciprian Ciuntu

The universe is of two types: the observable and the great unknown. The sacred can be seen as a part of the universe that people cannot see or understand.

The exact definition says that the sacred is a privileged area in which its originator manifests itself energetically and authentically to elaborate or stabilize a world, counteracting the inert. So, the sacred is everything and nothing at the same time because it can be demonstrated but not believed by all. People's faith is limited by the verb "to be," which refuses to accept that there is something after death, the situation being similar to the struggle between atheists and church people.

It would have been too easy to acquire the sacred by birth. Everything that is easily obtained is not appreciated for its true value. For this reason, for many people, finding that "something that is missing" takes a lifetime. People search but don't know what to find. Maybe we are not ready to reach that level of spirituality. Maybe we are too blinded by the banal to see that the sacred is in front of us.

For this reason, I believe that the eyes may see the beauty of the world, but this temporary world is not the one that nourishes our soul. That is why I believe that until our heart finds the missing element, it will travel through many places because each of us is different, which makes the Divinity different for all. The place where we will find it and the way it appears in our lives will fill that void that many feel.

Whether people believe in God, Allah, Buddha, other higher gods or spirits, or in nothing at all, the mystery that the sacred represents attracts them, even if there are already answers taken from other religions. Where do I meet the sacred? Maybe I don't know how to look for him. Maybe I've met him before, but I didn't know how to enjoy him. I consider that I am not yet ready to give up my prejudices and the things I believe in. But I trust that whatever is beyond childhood stories, paragraphs describing the Great Unknown, or Eliade's books, Divinity must not appear in our lives as a whirlwind that will break us from the reality in which we live.

"Search, and you will find" is one of the quotes that make us carry this journey.

We may find out what the sacred is. We may never find out. But in the meantime, as St. Augustine said, my soul burns because I want to know.

Snowflakes and People

Luminta-Elena Stoenescu

It was lightly snowing outside, and the trees were white. Everything was white.

I am looking forward to taking the skates out of the box again. Some people hurry to get inside and warm up, but I hurry to get to the rink in the schoolyard. It was getting dark, but the skating rink was lit up. The music urges you to go ahead and not stop. I've been skating for a few hours, and the cold is now gone. I feel fine. I'm skating again, around the rink and through the streets of this mountain town.

Now and then, I raise my head so the snowflakes touch my face. I feel a state of happiness that is difficult to describe. Winter is the season of joy and surprises of all kinds. I reach out to see the snowflakes melt in my hand, unique and unrepeatable snowflakes disappearing. I once read an article in a science magazine that said every snowflake has a different geometric configuration. In macro photography, cameras are used to enlarge each snowflake, making it easier to see their uniqueness and the harmony of geometric shapes.

Millions and billions of unique snowflakes come and go. Humans are like snowflakes, unique and unrepeatable. But unlike snowflakes which disappear when they give off heat, people blossom harmoniously with the warmth of love.

We linger for a while in this life, entering eternity with our thoughts and feelings. Our deeds are done, and we carry them into an absolute continuous present. Our time on earth is not absolute. We can measure it. It has a beginning and an end. God determines it. Eternity, however, is timeless. It has no beginning. It has no end. It is the present moment of fundamental dynamics. Eternity is not determined by something or someone.

God's creations know that no two people are alike. Not even twins are wholly identical because each has his or her unique DNA. Each has his or her own personality. We are unique and unrepeatable beings in human history. None of us has existed in the past and will not exist until the end of the ages, just like unique and unrepeatable snowflakes.

It is late. I walk into the warm atmosphere of my home. I feel tired, but fatigue does not bother me. Instead, it helps me to rest. In the morning, I start over cheerfully.

April

Asma Nooruddin

When my father completed his term in Afghanistan, we took a detour through Pakistan and India on our way to Bangladesh. We stayed in Islamabad for several days at a family friend's home. We loved it there. The city was lush and beautiful, and the climate was pleasant. Low walls separated the houses, which the children and cats used to climb onto and roam the entire neighborhood. Back then, it was safe to wander around without adult supervision.

Afterward, we took the train from Delhi to Calcutta. Delhi and Islamabad could not be more different. While Islamabad was a strikingly green and well-planned city, I only remember the smog and the concrete in Delhi. Because I was still very young, I dozed off through most of the journey. I have no recollection of stopping in Agra to see the Taj Mahal.

I do, however, remember our short stop in Patna. There, we visited my father's cousin. He had taxidermy of a big Royal Bengal tiger in his living room, which he hunted himself after it attacked a village. We children were so scared to pass by the fearsome tiger. I'm sure this terror is what made the stay so memorable.

Once the train reached its destination, we spent the day at the Calcutta Zoo. There, we saw a live Royal Bengal tiger along with a blue-eyed Siberian. From a safe distance away, I thought tigers were very noble creatures.

On the final leg of our journey, we took a flight from Calcutta to Dhaka. We were served a three-layered cake colored green, red, and white to match the airlines during our flight. It was so delicious I craved it for years after that. Recently, one of my relatives told me it was a Savoy cake. I felt nothing short of excitement when he shared this piece of information. I bet if I were to try it now, it would taste as sweet as these childhood memories.

I was only seven years old when we moved from Afghanistan to Bangladesh, right before foreign powers invaded Kabul. Thus, my experiences were never tainted by the war and destruction of these beautiful countries. I pray that when peace returns, the beauty I once knew can be restored.

Friends

Angelina Nădejde

After God created the world
he did not rest until he invented
friendship.

He knew we would sometimes be
single-winged birds
struggling helplessly to fly
to greater heights.

And then they, our friends,
are the visible angels who offer us
their wings.
They kneel beside us,
they hold us in their arms
as God holds the earth in his hands.

They wipe our tears with white kerchiefs
edged with hope,
the gentle touches are breezes of the wind
in spring

and their hugs have
soul perfume.

It helps us get up,
and they pray in secret
for us be well.

A New Beginning

Em Sava

She got out of bed and opened the blinds. The roofs of the houses greeted her with snow, domestic, like good soldiers, retiring. She washed her face with cold water and looked in the mirror. She was tired, though she had slept for almost eight hours. She sighed softly. The clock read 6:43 a.m. Another pointless day.

She thought about the mantras on her friend's bathroom mirror and smiled wryly. *You're beautiful! You're smart! I love you!*

She did not believe in such nonsense. The years had overshadowed her beauty, and her intelligence had gaps like a wire mesh. Her choices confirmed to her that she was not very smart.

She climbed into the shower. The hot water lifted her spirits a little. She put on the coffee. She dressed in absent movements. There was an oppressive sadness in her. The house roared like an orphaned wolf in the woods. Loneliness grinned in every corner.

As the coffee whispered in the kitchen, she turned on her heel and went to look intently in the mirror with hope. The eyes looking at her were sad. Encouragingly, she heard herself say, "You are healthy. You have a roof over your head and many days ahead. Get up! You can!" Sad eyes blinked back at her but in interest. Her words weren't persuasive, but she felt hope.

See? This is the beginning.

Fatigue nearly popped her like a soap bubble. She heard herself say, "You are beautiful. You are intelligent. I love you!"

She glanced at the mirror and threw a meringue at it. Then she laughed out loud.

It's time for a new beginning. Not tomorrow, not Monday, not next week, not on the first day of the month or at the beginning of the year, but right now, at 8:37 in the morning. But how?

She wondered to herself.

What gives you peace? Relaxation? Life shows up from time to time with stardust and scattered moments, splashes of divinity.

She looked around in amazement. The house looked just as sad, but hope was starting to blossom. She had found courage for a new beginning in her life. At 8:37, on a regular Saturday morning. Sadness had suddenly fallen off like dry lizard skin. She smiled broadly. She had so much to do. She looked in the mirror and whispered, convincing herself, "You are beautiful, you are intelligent, and I love you!"

Curiosity at the Creek

David M. Oancea

Remembering and reliving experiences from my childhood give me insight into what motivates me now and what I love to do most. Most of my memories are from the summertime, during a period in time when kids played outside for most of the day, unsupervised by their parents.

I would go home for lunch and dinner, but I mostly rode my bike to visit friends, participate in activities at the local park, hit a tennis ball against a brick wall, go fishing at the pond, and often meet my friend Danny at the creek.

It only took five minutes to ride my bike through the neighborhood next to the high school football stadium to the stream that ran under a bridge. I couldn't wait to see what I might find and catch.

Danny taught me to put a can or jar in the water before I lifted a rock. Crayfish often hide under rocks, and if I found one, I'd position the container behind the crawfish since it would attempt to escape by propelling itself backward. Minnows and tadpoles were the most common fish we observed. I look forward to when the tadpoles begin to sprout legs and develop into frogs. This process fascinated me! I could hardly wait to return a week later to see the progress and maybe even see baby frogs.

The other reason I loved to go to the creek was that I often saw and experienced things for the first time there. There was an aspect to the unknown dangers and having to make decisions on my own without the help of a friend or adult supervision that interested me.

Now, later in life, one of my favorite activities is observing nature. When I'm at a beach, it's not sunbathing or relaxing near the water that I enjoy most. Rather, I prefer to look for what the ocean deposits on the beach and search for the hidden natural treasures overlooked by most people.

Summer Rain

Ioan Rosu

During a summer night, I was awakened by the raindrops beating on the window, and when I went outside, I heard the dog barking in fear because of the thunder and lightning that pierced the sky. I went back home, and after a while, I continued to sleep, a little scared by the storm outside.

When I woke up, I saw that the fruit did not cause any damage in the morning. The dry earth swallowed the water, and the chickens nibbled on the frames of the water-soaked cloth.

It was a beautiful new summer day when all things were in place. The hens could see the frames and their beetles on, and the dog sat next to the cage, smelling the air.

The splashes of water on the rose petals were like a morning kiss for the day that had just begun.

The vegetable garden seemed greener and more lively, and through the vines, you could see the sun's rays shining in the raindrops hanging on the grapes.

All the tumult of the night passed. Life went back to its course. The plants showed their green color of many shades. The flowers in front of the house showed their vivid colors, making the courtyard look more beautiful than before. The animals enjoyed what nature left behind for all.

Meet the Authors

Alina Bejan

Alina has a degree in tourism from Academia de Studii Economic. She has owned a tourism agency since 1997 and ventured into other business opportunities. www.travelconsultancy.ro

Ana Maria Rosu

Ana Maria is a fourth-grade student. She loves animals, and for that, she wants to become a zoologist. She plays tennis, loves to read, and enjoys nature.

Anastasia Ciuntu

Anastasia is a high school student interested in deciphering the languages. She is interested in pursuing a writer's career as an advocate for speaking her mind and promoting change.

Andrei Cristian Mateescu

Andrei is an eighth-grade student at Colegiul National George Enescu in Romania, where he studies pan flute and piano.

Angelina Nădejde

Angelina is a chemist engineer, married with three children and one granddaughter. She is a published author of three volumes of poems in the Romanian Language: Suflet la Oferta, 2014; Sunt un alt Anotimp, 2017; Intrebarile Mariutei, 2019.

Asma Nooruddin

Asma is a mother of three and the founder of Arizona Trade Network. **https://www.arizonatradenetwork.com**. She also works regularly with MOVE. **https://www.mvofa.org**

Bassam Matar

Bassam is a native of the African continent but was raised in Lebanon. He came to the United States as a teenager, and in college, he met his future wife. He studied to become an engineer and a college professor. He is a proud father of two.

Brenda Whillock

Brenda is a program coordinator for the Maricopa Community Colleges in the Workforce and Economic Development office. Her hobbies are most things outdoors, friends and conversation. The thing that brings her happiness is the love she has for God, her husband, and her four young children, who inspire her each day.

Chris Dorris

Chris is a Speaker, Author, Mental Toughness Coach, and Podcaster. **www.christopherdorris.com**

Ciprian Ciuntu

Ciprian is an Orthodox priest of 20 years. He is married and is a father of two. As a doctoral student at Alexandru I. Cuza University, he focused his studies on the history and impact of preaching. Part of his ministries is his continuous support for his children's education and his support of pro-life.

Cornel Todeasa

Cornel is an Orthodox priest for 40 years. Obtained his Doctor in Theology from University of Oradea in 2000. Since 2016 he enjoys retirement. He is an author of four books: Seek First the Kingdom;

Călătoria Bunătăților; Preacurata Maria, Scara Domnului Iisus; Așa L-am Cunoscut pe Părintele Arsenie, "Sfântul Ardealului."

Dacia Snider

Dacia was raised in Warren, OH. She attended Miami University and began her career in Cincinnati, OH. She currently lives near Geneva, Switzerland, with her husband Luke and two children, Ian and Elliana.

Dana Fodor Mateescu

Dana is a journalist who has worked for several Romanian newspapers since 1994. She is author for three books for children: Fetitele din Cimitirul Rosu; Inimioara de catel, Aventurile lui Baz-Baz, Regele cu coroana de hartie; and two books of short stories: Povestiri din Bucuresti, and Tembela pana la moarte si Norocosul.

David M. Oancea

David has worked with and served non-profit organizations in varied support and leadership capacities since completing academic studies at The College of Wooster, Wooster, Ohio (BA, Religious Studies) and St. Vladimir's Orthodox Theological Seminary, Yonkers, New York (M.Div.).

Elena Lupu

Elena has studied Communication and Public Relations and is working on her Master's in Advertising. She is a curious person who finds joy in new ideas, concepts, places, people, and experiences.

Em Sava

By her real name, Ela Mihu is a collaborator to various Romanian Publications and outside of Romania. She is the author of several books: Pasi, co-authored with Axel; Ana, a novel; one volume of poems, Fluturi si alte Frunza, and a short story's book Orizuru.

Emilian Ciprian Ene

Emilian is a life coach and author of the upcoming book: Feel and Grow Rich, together with Silviana Carter. He is co-founder of: www.bradulemotiilor.ro.

Eugen V. Rosu

Eugen has been an Orthodox priest for 30 years. He worked for a number of years as a hospital chaplain and university chaplain. He earned his Doctor of Ministry degree from South University. He enjoys tennis and walks in nature. He has a passion for church mission and pastoral ministry. **www.eugenrosu.com**

Felicia Ramirez-Perez

Felicia is a mother, wife, daughter, sister, and friend. She is a passionate and caring leader in Higher Education. Felicia lives in the Southwest and enjoys the outdoors. In her spare time, she enjoys movies and is an avid fisherwoman.

Ioan Rosu

Ioan is a high school student. He enjoys bicycling and soccer. He loves literature and history.

Kay Huber

Kay is a mother of three, grandmother of nine grandchildren, and five great-grandchildren. She enjoys her retirement in Minnesota.

Lori Foley-Jacquez

Lori is a Coordinator for the Computer Alliance of Hispanic Serving Institutions at Chandler-Gilbert Community College. In her free time, she likes to hike, teach exercise, and spend time with her grandchildren.

Luminita-Elena Stoenescu

She is a high school religion teacher. She is a graduate of the Polytechnic University of Timisoara and of the School of Letters, History, and Theology from the West University of Timisoara. She enjoys being with her children.

Mara Viliga

Mara is a graduate of the School of Economics and works in the tourism industry. Though traveling may be difficult, she finds refuge in books, which open new horizons.

Mariana Alexandrescu

Mariana is a mother of three and a graduate of Psychology and Ecology. She grew up in a Romanian Village painted with creative scenes of ineffable feelings, deep sprawled in her soul, which marked her soul trajectory.

Purvi Desai

Purvi is a mother of two. She earned a Bachelor & #39s degree in Finance from Pennsylvania State University. She worked for a Fortune 500 company for ten years until she decided to pursue a career with her health and wellness brand. She loves traveling, socializing, reading, and anything which brings calmness.

Răzvan Mateescu

Răzvan is a journalist, iconographer, and administrator of an online store with traditional Romanian Artifacts. **www.artizanescu.ro**

Ron Rock

Ron is retired after forty-seven years in healthcare as a paramedic and a nurse. He and his wife Nannette of forty years have three daughters and six grandchildren.

Silvia Grigore

Silvia is a legal journalist and author. She published three volumes ofpoems : Imposibilul din suflet; Fasii de Suflet; Suflet in zbor; and one novel, Pe facebook si in alta viata. She is interested in Orthodox Spirituality and traveling.

Silviana Carter

Silviana is an actress, life coach for children and parents, and author of the upcoming book " Feel and grow rich" with Ene Emilian. She is well known for the "Bradul Emotiilor Educational Center Online." **www.bradulemotiilor.ro**

Stamatoula P. Kretsedemas

Stamatoula is a mother of three, a grandmother of nine, and a great-grandmother of one. She loves her Greek Orthodox Church and her Hellenic dishes. She enjoys reading and the company of her family.

Vesna Lucic

Vesna is a designer and owner of Vesna Vestments and has been designing clothing as far as she remembers. Began making vestments with the spiritual guidance of Mother Epraksia-Nativity of the Mother of God Serbian Monastery, Indiana, in 2003.

http://www.vesnavestments.com/

We Appreciate Reviews!

If you have enjoyed what you have read, we invite you to share this book with others, and leave us a review!

https://amzn.to/3K0YEAy

Made in United States
North Haven, CT
14 October 2022